Advance Praise

"This book is a must read for every family law paralegal! It is so practical and helpful it should be in every paralegal's office and used to teach paralegal courses. I highly recommend it."

Lyne Ranson, founder of one of the largest family law firms in West Virginia. She taught paralegal courses at the University of Charleston for over 20 years and has regularly spoken at state and local paralegal conferences on a variety of topics. Lyne has been an attorney for 40 years serving as a circuit court judge, a federal white collar crime prosecutor, private practice, and an adjunct professor at the state law school training students in Trial Advocacy.

"Marks Chinn's and Janeah Sakalaukus Kerr's Paralegal Divorce Handbook *is a comprehensive and detailed guide for all family law paralegals. In fact, it might also be a valuable tool for new family lawyers as it provides a road map from initial consultation to completion of a trial. He includes not only practical tips but forms and checklists."*

Lynne Ustach, Past Co-Chair of the ABA Family Law Section Publications Board and recipient of the 2022 ABA Family Law Section Chair's award for meritorious service and loyalty exceeding what is expected of leadership.

"Mark and Janeah's book is a 'must read' for all family law paralegals and attorneys who collaborate with them. It provides useful, practical information and guidance about ways to improve the law practice for the benefit of all members of the legal team and their clients. I will certainly purchase this book and share it with all members of our law firm. I only wish the book was available earlier in my legal career."

Kathryn Smith Root, Senior Shareholder, Gevurtz Menashe, P.C., Portland, OR. Katherine is an ABA Family Law Section member and former Chair of ABA Family Law Section's International Law Committee. She received the Katherine O'Neil Volunteer Service Award from Oregon Women Lawyers and a Public Service Commendation from the United States Coast Guard for providing pro bono legal assistance to their service members for many years.

THE Divorce Paralegal Handbook

Mark A. Chinn
Janeah S. Kerr

ABA
AMERICAN BAR ASSOCIATION
Family Law Section

Cover design by Mary Anne Kulchawik/ABA Design

Printed in the United States of America.

27 26 5 4 3 2

Library of Congress Cataloging-in-Publication Data
Names: Chinn, Mark A., author. | Kerr, Janeah S., author.
Title: The divorce paralegal handbook / Mark A. Chinn, Janeah S. Kerr.
Description: First edition. | Chicago : American Bar Association, Family Law Section, 2023. | Includes index. | Summary: "This manual is not intended to be an educational piece on substantive law and procedure. Such education falls in the realm of formal paralegal training and the training in individual law offices in the states. This manual is a "how to" on helping your lawyer navigate the administration of effective case and client management, document assembly, hearing, deposition, and trial preparation. Each chapter contains brief and to-the-point discussions of each area, usually with one or more forms or checklists to make things easy"— Provided by publisher.
Identifiers: LCCN 2023036744 (print) | LCCN 2023036745 (ebook) | ISBN 9781639053407 (paperback) | ISBN 9781639053414 (epub)
Subjects: LCSH: Divorce—Law and legislation—United States—Handbooks, manuals, etc. | Divorce—United States—Handbooks, manuals, etc. | Legal assistants—United States—Handbooks, manuals, etc.
Classification: LCC KF535 .C45 2023 (print) | LCC KF535 (ebook) | DDC 346.7301/66—dc23/eng/20230914
LC record available at https://lccn.loc.gov/2023036744
LC ebook record available at https://lccn.loc.gov/2023036745

Discounts are available for books ordered in bulk. Special consideration is given to state bars, CLE programs, and other bar-related organizations. Inquire at Book Publishing, ABA Publishing, American Bar Association, 321 N. Clark Street, Chicago, Illinois 60654-7598.

www.shopABA.org

Contents

Preface *vii*
Acknowledgments *ix*
About the Authors *xi*
ABA Publications *xiii*

Part 1 Introductory **1**
What Is a "Paralegal"? *2*
"Certification" *3*

Part 2 Administration **5**
Client Intake *6*
Intake Questionnaire *11*
Confidentiality *15*
Contact Information Management *18*
Setting Up a File *19*
Scheduling *20*
Taking Over a Case from Another Attorney *21*
Referral Source Thank You Letters *22*
Email Pitfalls *23*
Tips for Avoiding Breaches of Client Confidentiality *24*
The Asset List *26*
Instructing the Client on How to Send Documents *30*
What to Do with a Complaint *31*
Hearing Cancellation *36*
Sending Large Files *37*
Technology Resources *41*
When the Attorney Is Away *44*

Part 3 Document Preparation **45**
Correspondence *46*
Drafting Pleadings *47*
Pleadings Error Checklist *48*
Preparation of Financial Statements *49*
Checklist: Supporting Financial Documents and Related Information *53*
Divorce Agreement Completion Checklist *56*
Drafting a Divorce Agreement *57*
Entry of Agreed Divorce *60*
QDRO Basics *61*

Part 4 Discovery **67**
Discovery 68
Deposition Preparation Calendaring 71
Uniform Interstate Depositions and Discovery Act (UIDDA) 72
Bates Numbering Documents 79
Sample Bank Subpoena 85
Sample Cellular Carrier Subpoena 90
Sample Counseling Records Subpoena 94
Sample Deposition Subpoena 98
Sample Doctor Records Subpoena 100
Sample Employer Subpoena 104
Sample Notice of Deposition 108
Sample Notice of Inspection 110
Sample Notice of Supplemental Discovery 112
Sample Pharmacy Records Subpoena 114
Sample Police Department Records Subpoena 118
Sample Private Investigator Subpoena 122
Sample School Subpoena 126

Part 5 Trial **131**
The Temporary Hearing 132
Interim Trial Management 135
Calendaring for Trial Preparation 137
Trial Prep Checklist 138
The Checklists 141
Child Support Calculation 162
The Fact Sheet 163
Trial Preparation Overview 164
Trial Notebook Requirements 167
Making Sure Client and Witnesses Are Prepared for Trial 169
Evidentiary Tools for Trial 178
The "What We Want" Exhibit 185
Trial Exhibits 186
Prepare the Order before Court 187
What to Take to Trial 188
Tracking Trial Exhibits 189
Trial Diary 191

Index **193**

Select materials are available for download at https://www.ambar.org/DivPar

Preface

I have been obsessed with the management and mechanics of law practice from the very beginning of my career. This obsession probably started with my mechanical engineer father, who always had a system for how he worked. Later, I worked in a railroad factory where the workers there—mostly immigrants from Italy, Germany, Greece, and Hungary—taught me how to work systematically and safely. As a lawyer, I employed the assistance of law firm coaches from the Atticus Law Practice Management team from Orlando, Florida, who worked with me to examine my practice and systemize my procedures to avoid malpractice and increase efficiency.

This manual is written by a family lawyer for family law paralegals. The genesis for the book was a successful seminar for paralegals staged by the Family Law Section (FLS) in 2022 under the leadership of then–FLS Chair Candace Peeples of Birmingham, Alabama. The publications board determined that the resounding success of the program merited further work in the area of supporting paralegals in family law.

This manual is not intended to be an educational piece on substantive law and procedure. Such education falls in the realm of formal paralegal training and the training in individual law offices in the states. This manual is a "how to" on helping your lawyer navigate the administration of effective case and client management, document assembly, hearing, deposition, and trial preparation. Each chapter contains brief and to-the-point discussions of each area, usually with one or more forms or checklists to make things easy.

Acknowledgments

For this book, I would like to acknowledge my associate, Janeah Kerr, who has worked with me for the last many years to build forms and place them in our document assembly programs. Every time we do something new, we try to standardize it and place it in the system. We are always examining trial preparation and trial mechanics and refining our skills.

I have used materials generated for the paralegal seminar by the following:

- Melissa J. Avery, Indianapolis, IN, Financial Affidavits
- Missy DeArk, Louisville, KY, and Lyne Ranson, Charleston, WV, Tips for Finding Every Hidden Penny
- Adam J. Turbowitz, Hollywood, FL, and Jessica Kirk Drennan, Birmingham, AL, Discovery
- Emily W. McBurney, Atlanta, GA, QDRO Basics for Paralegals

Finally, to my wife, Cathy, who has been there with me and supported me through more than 40 years of law practice.

About the Authors

Mark Chinn has been married to Cathy for more than 40 years, and they have four daughters and four grandchildren and counting. Mark operates a firm that serves clients exclusively in the field of family law throughout the state of Mississippi.

He is the author of three American Bar Association (ABA) books:

- *How to Build and Manage a Family Law Practice,*
- *The Constructive Divorce,* and
- *Forms, Checklists, and Procedures for the Family Lawyer.*

He has been a frequent speaker for the ABA Family Law Section, The American Academy of Matrimonial Lawyers, state bar associations, and the Mississippi Bar on issues of family law practice management, marketing, and delivering world-class service.

Mark has received the following distinctions:

- Lawyer of the Year for his geographic area in Family Law, Best Lawyers of America
- Best Law Firms in Mississippi, U.S. News & World Report
- Top Ten Attorney Award, National Academy of Family Law Attorneys
- Best Family Law Firm in Mississippi, *Corporate INTL* Magazine
- Best Family Law Firm—Mississippi, CorpAmerica Legal Elite, 2016
- Mid-South Super Lawyers
- The Best Lawyers in America
- Martindale-Hubbell's Bar Register of Preeminent Lawyers

Mark was the recipient in 2014 of the Lawyers Citizenship Award, the Pro Bono Lawyer of the Year Award in 2011, and the 1996 Award of Merit presented by the Mississippi Bar.

Mark has been Chair of the Family Law Section of the Mississippi Bar twice and a member of the governing council of the Family Law Section of the ABA for two terms. He has served for many years on the Family Law Section Publications board.

Mark received his law degree from the University of Mississippi in 1978. He is admitted to practice in all courts in Mississippi, the Fifth and Seventh Circuits, and the U.S. Supreme Court.

Janeah Kerr is a native of Pass Christian, Mississippi. She graduated from Mississippi State University in 2013 with a Bachelor of Science in Kinesiology. She received her Juris Doctorate from Mississippi College School of Law in 2016. She has been working with Chinn & Associates, specializing in family law, since passing the Mississippi Bar in 2016.

ABA Publications

The following ABA Family Law publications provide additional resources for both attorneys and paralegals. These books may be purchased at ababooks.org:

- *The Divorce Trial Manual*, by Steven N. Peskind
- *The 1040 Handbook*, by Jack Zuckerman and Ron Thompson
- *The Forensic Accounting Deskbook*, by Miles Mason, Sr.
- *The Complete QDRO Handbook*, by Patricia Shewmaker and James R. Lewis
- *How to Build and Manage a Family Law Practice*, by Mark A. Chinn
- *Forms, Checklists, and Procedures for the Family Lawyer*, by Mark A. Chinn

Part 1

Introductory

What Is a "Paralegal"?

The current ABA definition of "paralegal" was adopted at the February 2020 ABA Midyear meeting of the House of Delegates and reads as follows:

> A paralegal is a person, qualified by education, training or work experience who is employed or retained by a lawyer, law office, corporation, governmental agency or other entity and who performs specifically delegated substantive legal work for which a lawyer is responsible.

In a law firm setting, a paralegal's time spent on substantive legal work is billed to clients at market rates, similar to other professional staff, but at a lower rate than attorneys. The ability to charge for services distinguishes paralegals from other legal clerical staff.

Paralegals work under the direction of the attorney. They cannot give legal advice, set fees, or represent a client in court. Here are some examples of typical paralegal duties:

- Conduct client interviews and maintain general contact with the client
- Locate and interview witnesses
- Conduct investigations and statistical and documentary research
- Conduct legal research
- Draft legal documents, correspondence, and pleadings for approval by the attorney
- Summarize depositions, interrogatories, and testimony
- Attend executions of depositions, court, or other proceeding with the attorney
- Author and sign communications provided the paralegal status is clearly indicated and the correspondence does not contain independent legal opinions or advice

"Certification"

While legal assistants are not required to have official training or certification, many do. Assistants with formal training may be either "certified" or "certificated." It is important to know the distinction.

A "certified" paralegal is one who has successfully passed a rigorous certification exam offered by at least one of the three national paralegal organizations. With all three of these exams, eligibility requirements include education and experience. The three major organizations and the certifications of each are as follows:

- **National Association of Legal Assistants (NALA)**—offers the Certified Paralegal exam and the CP designation. Advanced certification is also available to earn the Advanced Certified Paralegal (ACP) designation (www.nala.org).
- **National Federation of Paralegal Associations (NFPA)**—offers the Paralegal Advanced Competency Examination (PACE) in order to become a Registered Paralegal (RP) (www.paralegals.org).
- **National Association of Legal Professionals (NALS)**—offers the Professional Paralegal (PP) exam and designation (www.nals.org).

A paralegal applicant may think he or she is "certified" but, in fact, is not. Instead of being certified, the candidate may have only an educational certificate.

Individuals with an educational certificate have completed a short course of study or a post-baccalaureate program. Usually, a certificate requires fewer educational hours than an associate or bachelor's degree. An educational certificate does not mean the individual is "certified" by a national certifying organization. It simply means the person has completed educational hours in a paralegal program of study.

Source: Tricia Nelson, ACP. Ms. Nelson has been a paralegal educator for over 25 years. She has been published in the *Mississippi Lawyer* and several national paralegal publications.

Part 2

Administration

Client Intake

The procedure for client intake is up to the lawyers, but you can assist the lawyers in developing the best procedures for you and the firm. Here are the steps in the process:

The Initial Call or Contact. Initial contact from potential clients can take several forms. It can be a call to the office, an email, a contact through the firm website, a call from a friend, or a drop in. This is what initial callers usually want to know:

What is the charge for taking on a case?

Is there a charge for the initial interview? People often think there should be no charge for the initial consultation. This may be caused by the proliferation of personal injury ads where they say they offer "free consultations."

Answers to questions they have. People often think they can call and just get a legal question answered.

The receptionist or phone answering service should have a script for handling these calls.

The script should be designed to advise prospective clients on the firm intake procedure, let them know how the firm charges, determine if the case is the type of case the firm handles, and obtain information that will allow for a conflict check before moving forward. Following is a sample script.

CHINN & ASSOCIATES, P.C.
TELEPHONE SCREENING FORM

Date: ___________________

Greeting: "Good morning/afternoon, Chinn & Associates, this is ____________, how may I help you?"

Determine: Is the caller a (circle)

Potential New Client
Current client
attorney
court personnel
other ______________________________

If any but potential new client, get name and number and brief description of what they need:.

Name:______________________
number: _____________________
Need: ________________________

If potential new client get the following:

CLIENT INFO.
Name: ______________________________

Address: ______________________________

____

Telephone: ______________________________

Who referred you to us? _____________________________

How can we help you? ____

____

Spouse or ex-spouse's name: _____________________________

Case Screening. Due to the need to manage conflicts, no significant contact should take place until a conflict check has taken place. Conflict checking can be the role of the receptionist or a legal assistant. The conflict check should be designed by the law firm lawyers but should make sure the firm has never represented the opposing party before.

Case Intake. Once a conflict check has been done, a script should be developed for beginning the intake process. The purpose of this contact is to obtain more detailed information about the case, explain the intake process, and make arrangements, if agreed, for the initial consultation.

Receptionist: Good Afternoon/Morning, I am calling for ________________.

Caller: response

Receptionist: How are you?/niceties, etc. My name is ________________ and I am calling from Chinn & Associates law firm. I received your message regarding (divorce or child custody). I am Mr. Chinn's legal assistant, so I cannot offer you any legal advice on this matter, but I was calling to set you up for an appointment with him.

Caller: response

Receptionist: First, has anything been filed in this matter?

- If so, get county and full legal names

Typically, the first thing we do is set people up for a brief phone call assessment with Mr. Chinn to ask any general questions you may have about the process. This phone call with him is $500.00, which includes setting up your file in our office, and payment of this fee also means that Mr. Chinn is prohibited from representing opposing parties in this matter, so he is "conflicted out" At the conclusion of that call, you will have the option to set up a full, in-person assessment with Mr. Chinn. In this meeting, you will go over your specific case with Mr. Chinn and create a strategy for going forward. The full assessment is $1,000.00.

Caller: allow them to respond/ask questions.

Receptionist: I would also like to talk to you about fees. Our firm operates on what are known as "flat fees", meaning that Mr. Chinn will quote you a fee for the entirety of your legal process during the assessment. We do not charge by the hour like many firms do.

Caller: allow for questions.

Receptionist: If all of this sounds alright to you, I would like to confirm your email address and send you our standard scheduling email. This email will contain all of the information we just went over, along with available day and times for assessments. Please let me know which, if any, of the appointment slots work for you. If none of the times are convenient for you, let me know and we can work together to find a better time. Also, this email will have a secure link to pay for your assessment, and we will secure your spot on our calendar upon payment. Lastly, please take a few minutes to fill out the questionnaire attached to the email. It asks for general information so that I may set up your file beforehand.

Do you have any other questions for me at this time?

Thank you, I will get that email sent to you right now.

Tips.

1. Don't bother with calls from people other than the client. If a client does not have the interest to make her or his own call, the call is likely a waste of time. Moreover, conflict and confidentiality issues arise from dealing with someone other than the client.
2. Don't give out legal information of any kind.
3. Do not schedule a consultation unless a payment method is secured.
4. If the client is involved in litigation, have him or her provide the pleadings or the case number in advance.
5. Develop a standard client questionnaire for the new client to fill out that provides all of the basic information necessary for file setup and for document assembly. We have created such a form using Adobe Acrobat that allows the client to fill out the questionnaire in advance and email it in.

Intake Questionnaire

First Name: ______________________ Last Name: ______________________

Email Address: ____

Please enter an address where you would feel comfortable receiving mail from us. If you would not like to receive mail, type "NO MAIL."

Address: ____

City: ______________________ State: ________ Zip: ____________

Please enter the address of your marital home. No mail will be sent to this address unless it is the same as above.

Address: ____

City: ______________________ State: ________ Zip: ____________

County: ____

Client's Information

Cell Phone Number: ____

Home Phone Number: ____

Office Phone Number: ____

Social Security Number: ____

Date of Birth: ____

Gender: ____

Place of Employment: ____

Your Annual Compensation: ____

Highest Level of Education: ____

Spouse/Adverse Party Information

Full Name: ____________________

Cell Phone Number: ____________________

Email Address: ____________________

Social Security Number: ____________________

Date of Birth: ____________________

Gender: ____________________

Place of Employment: ____________________

Their Annual Compensation: ____________________

Highest Level of Education: ____________________

Children's Information

Child 1 Full Name: ____________________

Child 1 Date of Birth: ____________________

Child 1 School: ____________________

Child 2 Full Name: ____________________

Child 2 Date of Birth: ____________________

Child 2 School: ____________________

Child 3 Full Name: ____________________

Child 3 Date of Birth: ____________________

Child 3 School: ____________________

Child 4 Full Name: ____________________

Child 4 Date of Birth: ____________________

Child 4 School: ____________________

Child 5 Full Name: ______________________________

Child 5 Date of Birth: ______________________________

Child 5 School: ______________________________

List every place where the CHILDREN have lived for the past FIVE (5) years starting with the most recent address. You must include the dates and people who resided in the home with the child.

Address: ______________________________

City: ____________________ State: ________ Zip: ____________

Approximate date children started living there? ____________________

Who resides in the home? ______________________________

What is their relation to the children? ____________________

Previous Residence #1

Address: ______________________________

City: ____________________ State: ________ Zip: ____________

Approximate date children started living there? ____________________

Who resided in the home? ______________________________

What is their relation to the children? ____________________

Previous Residence #2

Address: ______________________________

City: ____________________ State: ________ Zip: ____________

Approximate date children started living there? ____________________

Who resided in the home? ______________________________

What is their relation to the children? ____________________

Previous Residence #3

Address: ______________________________

City: ______________________ State: ________ Zip: ____________

Approximate date children started living there? ______________________

Who resided in the home? ______________________________

What is their relation to the children? ______________________________

Has custody of the children ever been an issue in any court of law? ____________

Is there anyone other than the parents who could claim right to custody of or visitation with the children? ______________________________

Is the wife currently pregnant? ______________________________

Date of Marriage: ______________________________

Where did you obtain your marriage license? ______________________

Date of Separation: ______________________________

Where were you living at the time of separation? ______________________

Are there any upcoming hearing/trial dates? ______________________

Is an answer due to a complaint or discovery requests? ________________

Is there an appeal time running or a statute of limitations? ______________

Critical dates in your case? ______________________________

How did you find out about [Firm Name/Attorney] ? ________________

____

Confidentiality

The confidentiality rules for lawyers apply to the lawyer's entire staff. Paralegals must be acutely aware of these rules.

There are two related bodies of law covering the fundamental principle of confidentiality of information in an attorney-client relationship. The first is the Attorney-Client Privilege (which includes the attorney work-product doctrine) that is found in the law of evidence. The second body of law is the Rule of Confidentiality that is established in the rules of professional conduct for attorneys.

The Attorney-Client Privilege

The attorney-client privilege applies in judicial proceedings in which the attorney is a witness or in which the attorney is required to produce evidence regarding a client. The privilege attaches to communications from the attorney to the client, as well as to communications to the attorney from the client. The attorney-client privilege is afforded only to *confidential* communications between the attorney and the client. To be confidential, the communication must not be *intended* to be disclosed to a third person other than those to whom the disclosure is made in order to provide legal services to the client, such as the attorney's associates and other staff. (An eavesdropper would not be able to testify about communication that is otherwise subject to the privilege, since a third person's eavesdropping is not a breach of confidentiality, because that disclosure was not intended.) If a communication between an attorney and a client is made in the presence of someone else, such as a friend or family member of the client's, then it would not be considered to be confidential. Likewise, communications between an attorney and a client that are made in a public place would not normally be intended to be confidential and therefore generally do not fall under the privilege.

The privilege belongs to the client, who may prevent an attorney's disclosure of confidential information as a witness or of production of evidence in a legal proceeding regarding the client. No privilege attaches to communications between an attorney and a client where the following is true:

1. Such communication is in furtherance of the commission of a crime or fraud.
2. Two or more persons are claiming the privilege on behalf of a deceased client.
3. Issues of breach of duty arise in a dispute between the attorney and the client.
4. The communication is regarding a document attested as a witness by the attorney.
5. The communication was relevant to joint clients, and it is being offered in a legal action between the joint clients.

Rule of Confidentiality

This ethical duty of confidentiality applies to *all other situations* than those just covered where evidence is sought from an attorney through compulsion of law. An attorney may not disclose confidential client information except as authorized by the client or as required under the Rules of Professional Conduct for attorneys. This ethical duty exists no matter who else knows the information that is confidential. Information that should not be disclosed includes that which the attorney has reason to believe may be detrimental to a client or which the client has requested not be disclosed. This duty exists even after an attorney's representation of a client has ended.

Authorized disclosures of otherwise confidential information are implied under the rules of professional conduct where they are necessary to carry out the representation of a client. This implied waiver of disclosure of confidential information should be covered in the attorney-client contract, wherein clients acknowledge that the attorneys and staff of the law firm will be required to investigate matters by contacting witnesses, issuing subpoenas, and exchanging information regarding cases. The contract should further explain that at times the attorneys and staff may reveal information about the client that may ordinarily be privileged. For example, an attorney may have to tell a witness about a client's claims or circumstances in order to obtain the witness's perspective. The contract should also state that the client waives confidentiality rules and the attorney-client privilege in order to allow the attorney to perform the requested legal work properly. Any exceptions to this waiver must be stated by a client in writing. The attorney may also obtain confidential information about a client from witnesses and other sources such as counselors, ministers, priests, and physicians, if necessary, for proper preparation of a case.

Furthermore, under the Rules of Professional Conduct an attorney may disclose information by admitting a fact that cannot be properly disputed or in settlement negotiations where disclosure may be necessary to facilitate a satisfactory conclusion. The rules also allow lawyers within a firm to disclose confidential information regarding a client to each other.

There are limited exceptions to the ethical rules regarding an attorney's duty to keep certain information confidential:

1. An attorney may not counsel or assist a client in conduct that is criminal or fraudulent.

2. Confidential information may be used by an attorney to establish a claim or defense on his or her own behalf in a controversy between the attorney and the client, in a civil or criminal matter involving the attorney for conduct in which the client was involved, or in response to allegations in any proceeding concerning the attorney's representation of the client.

3. An attorney may reveal confidential information regarding a client to the extent required by law or court order.

(There are other exceptions to this ethical rule regarding matters within the bar membership that do not normally apply to an attorney-client relationship.)

The previously listed exceptions to confidentiality rules allude to the companion Rule of Professional Conduct, which prevents attorneys from using false evidence. For example, if an attorney has knowledge that information in a client's answer to discovery is fraudulent, **the attorney may not allow the client to respond to the discovery in a fraudulent manner.** Nor may attorneys allow a client or other witness to testify falsely (that would be suborning perjury) or otherwise knowingly present false evidence at a trial or any stage of litigation. **The upshot of this rule is that if a client discloses something to the attorney and such information is requested in a legitimate discovery response, the privilege does not apply and the information must be provided.** For example, if a client were to confess to her or his lawyer that her or his income was really much greater than represented, the attorney must disclose the correct information; the attorney may not allow a lie or misinformation to take place in response to an appropriate request.

Moreover, if a lawyer has offered evidence of material importance that is later learned to be false, the attorney must take reasonable measures to remedy the situation. Such remedial action should include attempting to persuade a client to take suitable action or, failing that, to seek to withdraw from further representation of the client in the matter.

Contact Information Management

It is helpful to the attorneys if staff is cognizant of keeping accurate contact information in the files.

Double-check that the client information is complete in the system. If a change in information becomes evident, make the changes in the file and make sure the changes translate to document merger software.

Take initiative in making sure all persons related to a file are maintained in the file. Contact information should be included for the following types of persons:

- Opposing counsel (in addition, if opposing counsel has a legal assistant, place him or her in the file)
- Judge assigned to the case
- Court administrator
- Witnesses
- Experts

Setting Up a File

Procedures for setting up a file vary from firm to firm, and they vary based upon whether case management software is used and whether the firm is "paperless." However, these are the basics of file setup:

1. Insert contact information of the client, the opposing party, the opposing attorney, the judge, and the court administrator.
2. Determine the referral source and indicate that in the file. Good practice is to keep up with referrals and to thank the source.
3. Place a basic summary of the case in the file, including length of marriage, occupations and incomes of the parties, names and ages of the children, basic asset descriptions, and the issues. (This is likely to be done by the attorney during intake.)
4. Double check conflicts just to make sure.
5. Check whether there has been a fee understanding and payment of a fee or retainer. Best practices call for a written contract or memorandum of understanding to be completed in each new matter.
6. Determine if any dates for hearings or responses should be calendared.

Scheduling

A key function for the paralegal is scheduling.

Before scheduling ask for details on the matter to be scheduled, whether it be a hearing, a deposition, or a trial. These are some of the things you need to know:

1. How long will the hearing or trial take?
2. What time interval is needed for scheduling? For example, if a hearing is to be scheduled, are there things that need to take place in the interim? How far off does the attorney want it scheduled, or does the attorney want it scheduled as soon as possible?
3. If the matter is a hearing, does the hearing require a court reporter to be available?

Work with your attorney to develop a specific list of rules to follow when scheduling. Following is a sample list developed over the many years of my practice.

1. Do not schedule before 9:30 A.M. This gives the attorney time to get in and get her or his day started and to properly prepare for the appointment.
2. Do not schedule appointments back to back. This gives the attorney time to prepare for the second appointment.
3. Do not schedule afternoon appointments until 1:30. This prevents clients showing up early when the reception area is closed and prevents the attorney from being late for appointments because of lunch delays.
4. Do not schedule appointments after 4:00 P.M. This ensures that staff is available for the appointment and that things do not go too late at night. Of course, if there is good reason to schedule a late afternoon appointment, take that to your attorney before scheduling.
5. Where possible, do not schedule hearings on Mondays. This prevents weekend work and makes it easier to prepare.
6. When scheduling trials, check the days before and after to make sure that scheduling is not congested, which leads to improper preparation and panic-driven work.

Taking Over a Case from Another Attorney

There is not a more dangerous activity than taking a file over from a previous lawyer. The danger is extremely high in the first 24 to 48 hours. The reason is that one can never be sure that something is not supposed to happen in that period. In addition, there has been a full set of activities for which your firm has not been responsible that has set the framework in which you are to operate. Procedures that you might have implemented along the way—such as issuing a standard set of discovery at the outset—have probably not been done. At the outset be careful and follow the checklist to minimize the danger.

Checklist for Taking a File Over from Another Lawyer

1. Investigate online docket or call clerk of court to determine what pleadings are on file. Is an answer due to anything, and, if so, when?
2. The original court file is to be obtained immediately, either online or from the clerk. Clients and other attorneys are not to be trusted with providing you with accurate information, although you can certainly request this from them until you can double check the actual file.
3. As much of the file as possible is to be obtained from the client or previous counsel. This is not to be relied upon but is to be used only as needed.
4. An entry of appearance and/or motion and order substituting counsel is to be sent for filing and to opposing counsel immediately to ensure pleadings must be copied to you.
5. Previous counsel is to be contacted to determine
   - the status of pleadings;
   - inside information; and
   - whether anything is due.
6. Previous counsel is to be written to confirming information received and notifying him or her that you are relying upon his or her information.

Referral Source Thank You Letters

Personal referrals of business are the best source of business for most family law lawyers. You can assist your lawyer with her or his in-person marketing by doing the following things under her or his supervision.

1. Always find out how a new case came to the firm. Build that question into the new client intake script and the new client questionnaire.
2. Keep track of the referral sources using case management systems. Calendar dates for keeping up with the referral source via email, phone, lunch, or drinks.
3. Help your attorney develop and keep a list of the top 25 referral sources.
4. Develop a holiday gift list.
5. **Always have your attorney send a personal thank you to referral sources.**

Email Pitfalls

Much of our communication today is via email. One of the benefits of email is speed. However, the speed of emails also creates the danger of mistakes. Here are some common email errors:

- Wrong name goes into email due to autofill. Double check who your email is going to.
- "Reply all" is used, leading to the wrong people being copied. Be very careful of reply all. A big error is to accidentally communicate with an opposing party using reply all. The opposing counsel may have copied his or her client on the email, so when you hit reply all, your communication will go to the opposing party, which would be a technical ethical violation.
- Email thread. Be careful sending emails off of emails you have received. An entire thread of emails might accompany your email. This could lead to many issues, including inadvertently sending a confidential client communication to the opposing party.
- Attachment not provided. Double check before you send an email to make sure you attach the document you said you were attaching. If you have Outlook, this issue can easily be fixed by enabling the option "Warn me when I send a message that may be missing an attachment." This feature in Outlook is located in File > Options. Select the Mail section of the Outlook Options window. Scroll down to the "Send messages" feature and make sure this option is checked.
- Autocorrect could insert a word you do not intend to use. Proofread your emails the way you would an important letter. If you have Outlook, autocorrect can be enabled or disabled with the option "Always check spelling before sending." This feature in Outlook is located in File > Options. Select the Mail section of the Outlook Options window. Scroll down to the "Compose messages" feature.

Tips for Avoiding Breaches of Client Confidentiality

By Michael A. Mosberg, Esq., New York, NY

Best Practices for Paralegals Related to Privilege

- Always copy your attorney on all your direct written communications with a client.
- If you're relaying a message from your attorney, or your email contains or requests any information that is privileged or protected, it's a good practice to reference PRIVILEGED COMMUNICATION in your subject line.
- Use caution in copying third parties on any communications with clients, as this could risk waiving privilege. The rule of thumb is that a client's family members and/or agents are usually not covered by privilege, whereas an attorney's agents and employees are usually covered by privilege.
- Be very careful about the email autocomplete address function, as this is a very common source of inadvertently misdirected confidential emails. Consider turning it off!
- Identify your memoranda or other written reports to your attorney describing your activities or research as "Work Product Prepared at Attorney's Request" or any words to that effect.
- Take extra care with preparing document productions in discovery. It often falls to paralegals and other staff to ensure that privileged documents are not inadvertently disclosed in production.
- If you do find that a privileged document has been produced, bite the bullet and inform your supervising attorney immediately. Delay in notifying your opposing counsel of the inadvertent disclosure could result in a waiver of privilege as to the disclosed material.

Practical Tips for Protecting Client Confidences

- Don't discuss work outside of work. As tempting as it may be to talk about work with colleagues, friends, and family, client confidences must not be revealed, even hypothetically. With regard to communications outside the office, members of the legal team should never discuss clients or cases at home or in social settings, including on social media and online professional networks. Additionally, discussing clients or cases with coworkers outside the office should be avoided in the event such conversations could be overheard.
- Be cognizant of your surroundings when communicating with clients, even in the office. Even brief in-person conversations with clients should be conducted in a conference room or office with the door closed, not in the lobby, hallway, or

elevator. When speaking with or about a client or a case by phone, the door to the office should be closed and the use of the speakerphone should be avoided. A call from or about a client should certainly not be taken with another client or third party present.

- Arrange individual offices to avoid opportunities for visitors to inadvertently or intentionally observe or obtain confidential client information. Files on the desk or other furniture should be kept closed. Computer monitors should be positioned so they are not in the line of vision of visitors in the office or passersby. Password-protected screen savers prevent others from viewing client information in the user's absence. Mail should be kept in a closed folder, not open on the desk or within view. Individual offices and work areas should be separated from the lobby and conference room areas by a closed door.
- Implement strict electronic data policies. If client information is stored in a computer database, access to that database must be controlled. Computer passwords should be periodically changed and should not be written down in the office. If members of the legal team take client files, flash drives, or laptops containing client information outside the office, policies should be established for securing those files and computers. Mobile phones and tablets used for work or client communication should be protected by a passcode or fingerprint recognition. Find-my-device apps should be installed to recover lost devices. When any computer device is no longer used, the hard drive or other storage component must be removed or wiped before returning, donating, or otherwise discarding the hardware.
- All wastepaper must be shredded. This is not overkill. Shredding is essential to avoid disclosure of client information. Your shredding machine or service must utilize a cross-shredding feature to ensure the obliteration of all information. No wastepaper should leave the premises intact.
- Use faxes, email, and texts with caution and attention. While faxing, emailing, and even texting client information is not necessarily a violation of client confidentiality, errors in sending such electronic communications can lead to serious consequences. Sending sensitive client information by fax, email, or text message should be avoided whenever possible. When using faxes, call ahead to confirm the number and ensure that the intended recipient is available to receive it. Faxes should be prominently marked confidential and should request that the recipient call the sender to confirm receipt. As with faxes, email addresses and mobile numbers should be confirmed prior to use, and messages should be set up to generate a return receipt. It is also important to include a prominent confidentiality statement in the text of client-related email messages. Clients who wish to communicate with the law office electronically should be advised of the lack of a guarantee of security and should be advised against transmittal of sensitive information by such means. Keep in mind that even if all of these precautions are taken, the lawyer is responsible for even accidental revelation of confidential client information.

The Asset List

Attorneys need tools to digest large amounts of information. This is particularly true with the assets and liabilities of the marriage. The "asset list" is a tool to put all of the assets and liabilities on one page for the attorney to calculate what an appropriate division might be. This can be done in a simple work document, but the best asset lists are done using Microsoft Excel or Adobe Acrobat. A first-class asset list identifies the source and date of the value. If the parties differ on what the value of assets are or whether an asset is marital or nonmarital, a five-star asset list will identify the respective positions of the parties.

Set forth here is a simple asset list and division:

	Description of Asset/Liability	**Value**
Real Estate		
#1	**[Address of Real Property]**	
	Appraisal of Real Property	$350,000.00
	Outstanding Mortgage Balance	($257,000.00)
	Net Value of Real Property	$93,000.00
	Total Real Property	**$93,000.00**
Bank Accounts		
#2	Wife's Checking Account 1234	$12,500.00
#3	Husband's Checking Account 5678	$567.00
#4	Joint Savings Account 9012	$475.00
	Total Bank Accounts	**$13,542.00**
Retirement		
#5	Husband's IRA 7832	$50,000.00
#6	Wife's Roth IRA 9274	$35,000.00
#7	Wife's 401(k)	$6,000.00
	Total Retirement	**$91,000.00**
Vehicles		
#8	Audi A7, 102,000 Miles	$30,000.00
	Vehicle Loan	($2,300.00)
	Net Value of Audi A7	$27,700.00
#9	2019 Infinity QX80, 60,000 Miles	$50,000.00
	Vehicle Loan	($30,575.00)
	Net Value of 2019 Infinity QX80	$19,425.00
	Total Vehicles	**$47,125.00**
Boats		
#10	2007 Sea Ray Boat	$25,000.00
	Total Boats	**$25,000.00**
Household Items		
#11	Household Furniture	$20,000.00
#12	Workout Equipment	$1,500.00
	Total Household Items	**$21,500.00**
Credit Cards		
#13	Wife's Credit Card 6709	($6,500.00)
	Total Credit Card Debt	**($6,500.00)**
TOTAL ASSETS		**$284,667.00**

Set forth next is an asset and liability list with competing values of the parties. This puts the different positions of the parties on one page and is a good tool for evaluation by the attorney.

	Husband's Document	Wife's Document	Description of Asset/Liability	Husband's Value	Wife's Value
Real Estate					
#1			**[Address of Real Property]**		
	Appraisal as of 5.30.21	Appraisal as of 2.25.22	Appraisal of Real Property	$350,000.00	$300,000.00
	Statement as of 6.1.21	Statement as of 5.1.22	Outstanding Mortgage Balance	($257,000.00)	($250,000.00)
			Net Value of Real Property	$93,000.00	$50,000.00
			Total Real Property	**$93,000.00**	**$50,000.00**
Bank Accounts					
#2	Statement as of 5.15.21	Statement as of 4.30.22	Wife's Checking Account 1234	$12,500.00	$643.00
#3	Statement as of 5.15.21	Statement as of 4.30.22	Husband's Checking Account 5678	$567.00	$14,789.00
#4	Statement as of 5.15.22	Statement as of 5.15.22	Joint Savings Account 9012	$475.00	$475.00
			Total Bank Accounts	**$13,542.00**	**$15,907.00**
Retirement					
#5	Statement as of 5.15.21	Statement as of 6.22	Husband's IRA 7832	$50,000.00	$75,000.00
#6	Statement as of 5.30.21	Statement as of 4.30.22	Wife's Roth IRA 9274	$35,000.00	$20,000.00
#7	Statement as of 5.2.21	Statement as of 4.1.22	Wife's 401k	$6,000.00	$2,000.00
			Total Retirement	**$91,000.00**	**$97,000.00**
Vehicles					
#8	Kelly Bluebook	Financial Statement 1.1.22	Audi A7, 102,000 Miles	$30,000.00	$27,500.00
	Statement 5.1.21	Statement 6.1.22	Vehicle Loan	($2,300.00)	($1,500.00)
			Net Value of Audi A7	$27,700.00	$26,000.00
#9	Kelly Buebook	Financial Statement 1.1.22	2019 Infinity QX80, 60,000 Miles	$50,000.00	$50,000.00
	Statement 6.1.22	Statement 5.2.21	Vehicle Loan	($30,575.00)	($43,000.00)
			Net Value of 2019 Infinity QX80	$19,425.00	$7,000.00
			Total Vehicles	**$47,125.00**	**$33,000.00**
Boats					
#10			2007 Sea Ray Boat	$25,000	$35,000
			Total Boats	**$25,000**	**$35,000**
Household Items					
#11	Financial Statement	Contents Appraisal 5.1.22	Household Furniture	$20,000.00	$15,000.00
#12	Financial Statement	None	Workout Equipment	$1,500.00	$3,500.00
			Total Household Items	**$21,500.00**	**$18,500.00**
Credit Cards					
#13	Statement 4.2.21	Statement 6.2.22	Wife's Credit Card 6709	($6,500.00)	($12,500)
			Total Credit Card Debt	**($6,500.00)**	**($12,500)**
			TOTAL ASSETS	**$284,667.00**	**$236,907.00**

			Husband's Value	Wife's Value
Husband's Proposed Separate Property				
#14	Two Handguns	Gifted from Father	$1,800.00	$1,800.00
#15	Family Silver	Inherited from Mother	$350.00	$350.00
	Total Separate Property to Husband		**$2,150.00**	**$2,150.00**
Wife's Proposed Separate Property				
#16	Art	Gift from Father	$1,800.00	$1,800.00
#17	Shotgun	Inherited from Grandfather	$350.00	$350.00
	Total Separate Property to Wife		**$2,150.00**	**$2,150.00**

Set forth below is an asset and liability list with competing values of the parties and your client's proposed division. This puts the differences of the positions on one page and is a good tool to present to the mediator or the court because it shows the different valuations but provides your client's proposed division.

	Husband's Document	Wife's Document	Description of Asset/Liability	Husband's Value	Wife's Value	Husband's Proposed Division: Husband	Husband's Proposed Division: Wife	Wife's Proposed Division: Husband	Wife's Proposed Division: Wife
Real Estate									
#1			**[Address of Real Property]**						
	Appraisal as of 5.30.21	Appraisal as of 2.25.22	Appraisal of Real Property	$350,000.00	$300,000.00				
	Statement as of 6.1.21	Statement as of 5.1.22	Outstanding Mortgage Balance	($257,000.00)	($250,000.00)				
			Net Value of Real Property	$93,000.00	$50,000.00				
			Total Real Property	**$93,000.00**	**$50,000.00**		$93,000.00		$50,000.00
Bank Accounts									
#2	Statement as of 5.15.21	Statement as of 4.30.22	Wife's Checking Account 1234	$12,500.00	$643.00	$6,250.00	$6,250.00	$321.50	$321.50
#3	Statement as of 5.15.21	Statement as of 4.30.22	Husband's Checking Account 5678	$567.00	$14,789.00	$283.50	$283.50	$7,394.50	$7,394.50
#4	Statement as of 5.15.22	Statement as of 5.15.22	Joint Savings Account 9012	$475.00	$475.00	$237.50	$237.50	$237.50	$237.50
			Total Bank Accounts	**$13,542.00**	**$15,907.00**				
Retirement									
#5	Statement as of 5.15.21	Statement as of 6.22	Husband's IRA 7832	$50,000.00	$75,000.00	$50,000.00		$58,500.00	$16,500
#6	Statement as of 5.30.21	Statement as of 4.30.22	Wife's Roth IRA 9274	$35,000.00	$20,000.00	$15,362.50	$19,637.50		$20,000.00
#7	Statement as of 5.2.21	Statement as of 4.1.22	Wife's 401k	$6,000.00	$2,000.00	$6,000.00			$2,000.00
			Total Retirement	**$91,000.00**	**$97,000.00**				
Vehicles									
#8	Kelly Bluebook	Financial Statement 1.1.22	Audi A7, 102,000 Miles	$30,000.00	$27,500.00				
	Statement 5.1.21	Statement 6.1.22	Vehicle Loan	($2,300.00)	($1,500.00)				
			Net Value of Audi A7	$27,700.00	$26,000.00	$27,700.00		$26,000.00	
#9	Kelly Buebook	Financial Statement 1.1.22	2019 Infinity QX80, 60,000 Miles	$50,000.00	$50,000.00				
	Statement 6.1.22	Statement 5.2.21	Vehicle Loan	($30,575.00)	($43,000.00)				
			Net Value of 2019 Infinity QX80	$19,425.00	$7,000.00		$19,425.00		$7,000.00
			Total Vehicles	**$47,125.00**	**$33,000.00**				
Boats									
#10			2007 Sea Ray Boat	$25,000	$35,000	$25,000		$35,000	
			Total Boats	**$25,000**	**$35,000**				
Household Items									
#11	Financial Statement	Contents Appraisal 5.1.22	Household Furniture	$20,000.00	$15,000.00	$10,000.00	$10,000.00		$15,000.00
#12	Financial Statement	None	Workout Equipment	$1,500.00	$3,500.00	$1,500.00		$3,500.00	
			Total Household Items	**$21,500.00**	**$18,500.00**				
Credit Cards									
#13	Statement 4.2.21	Statement 6.2.22	Wife's Credit Card 6709	($6,500.00)	($12,500)		($6,500.00)	($12,500)	
			Total Credit Card Debt	($6,500.00)	($12,500)				
			TOTAL ASSETS	**$284,667.00**	**$236,907.00**	**$142,333.50**	**$142,333.50**	**$118,453.50**	**$118,453.50**

			Husband's Value	Wife's Value
Husband's Proposed Separate Property				
#14	Two Handguns	Gifted from Father	$1,800.00	$1,800.00
#15	Family Silver	Inherited from Mother	$350.00	$350.00
	Total Separate Property to Husband		**$2,150.00**	**$2,150.00**
Wife's Proposed Separate Property				
#16	Art	Gift from Father	$1,800.00	$1,800.00
#17	Shotgun	Inherited from Grandfather	$350.00	$350.00
	Total Separate Property to Wife		**$2,150.00**	**$2,150.00**

Instructing the Client on How to Send Documents

There are right and wrong ways to scan and send documents. Some wrong ways include files that are sent in the wrong file format (like JPG!), documents that are blurry or partially cut off, and my personal favorite—pictures of documents that also capture the sender's hands and home in the background. Save yourself the trouble of receiving poorly scanned documents from clients by providing the client with clear instructions to scan documents with his or her smartphone or tablet.

Steps to Scan Documents with a Smartphone/Tablet

- Download the free application called "Adobe Scan" to your smartphone or tablet.
- Select "document" within the application and hold your device over the document you are attempting to scan. You do not need to take a picture, as the application will automatically "capture" the document when it is ready.
- Once captured, hit "continue" on the bottom right if the scanned document looks good (if not, hit "retake"). After you hit "continue," you will keep doing this for each subsequent page of that particular document.
- After scanning the last page, hit "continue," then click on the scanned pages at the bottom right of your screen (it should have the total number of scanned pages in a blue circle).
- Next, select "Save PDF" located in the upper right corner of your screen.
- To send the saved PDF, hit "share" followed by the option "Share a copy."
- You can now send a scanned copy of your document in PDF format to your intended recipient—whether that be via text message or email.

What to Do with a Complaint

When a complaint is received, follow these steps:

1. Scan the complaint into the system and file it and distribute the complaint to the proper attorney.
2. Verify the date of service. First information on service will come from the client, but this cannot be trusted. Look for a proof of service in the court file for verification.
3. Verify the type(s) of summons accompanying the complaint. There may be a summons to answer the complaint and there may also be a summons to a hearing date, such as a temporary hearing or restraining order. Take the following steps: ask the client, inspect the court file, contact the court clerk if necessary.
4. Calendar the answer date with a reminder about a week ahead of time. Calendar any hearing dates.
5. Prepare an Entry of Appearance for approval by the responsible attorney. The purposes of an Entry of Appearance are to make sure no action can be taken in the file without proper notice to the attorney and to create an obligation to send notice of default should there be a failure to file a timely answer.
6. Jurisdiction. Your attorney will have to make a determination of whether there is personal jurisdiction over the client before an Entry of Appearance is filed or an answer is filed.
7. Generate a form answer denying allegations for your attorney to use as a template for her or his answer and possible counterclaim.
8. Generate standard discovery for your attorney to use as a template for immediately filing proper discovery.

Practice Tip. It is good practice to serve at least standard discovery with every complaint and with every answer. If this procedure is religiously followed, the firm can be confident that basic due diligence of discovery is being done automatically in every case.

IN THE ___________ COURT OF ___________ COUNTY, ___________
___________ JUDICIAL DISTRICT

[NAME OF PLAINTIFF] **PLAINTIFF**

VS. **CAUSE NO. _______________**

[NAME OF DEFENDANT] **DEFENDANT**

ENTRY OF APPEARANCE AND MOTION FOR ADDITIONAL TIME

NOW INTO COURT comes [Attorney Name] and enters [his/her] appearance as counsel of record for the [Defendant/Plaintiff] and moves the Court for additional time in which to answer and in the meantime asserts a general denial to the allegations of the Complaint and an intent to defend the Complaint.

This the _____ day of ____________, [year].

Respectfully submitted,
[CLIENT'S NAME]

By: /s/Attorney Name
Attorney Name

Attorney Name
Firm Name
Address of Firm Line 1
Address of Firm Line 2
Telephone
Telecopier
Email Address
Attorneys for [Client Name]

CERTIFICATE OF SERVICE

The undersigned counsel does hereby certify that this day a true and correct copy of the foregoing instrument was delivered, via ________, to opposing counsel.

SO CERTIFIED, this the _____ day of ____________, [year].

/s/Attorney Name
Attorney Name

IN THE ___________ COURT OF ___________ COUNTY, ___________
___________ JUDICIAL DISTRICT

[NAME OF PLAINTIFF] **PLAINTIFF**

VS. **CAUSE NO. _______________**

[NAME OF DEFENDANT] **DEFENDANT**

ANSWER TO COMPLAINT FOR DIVORCE

COMES NOW, **[CLIENT FULL NAME]**, ("Client First Name"), the Defendant, and files [his/her] Answer against the Plaintiff, [Opposing Party Full Name], ("Opposing Party First Name"), and in support thereof would show unto the Court the following facts, to wit:

ANSWER

1. Denied.
2. Denied.
3. Denied.
4. Denied.
5. Denied.
6. Denied.
7. (a.) Denied.
   (b.) Denied.

RELIEF SOUGHT

8. (a.) Denied.
   (b.) Denied.
   (c.) Denied.
   (d.) Denied.
   (e.) Denied.
   (f.) Denied.
   (g.) Denied.

TEMPORARY RELIEF SOUGHT

9. (a.) Denied.

 (b.) Denied.

 (c.) Denied.

 (d.) Denied.

 (e.) Denied.

 (f.) Denied.

10. Denied.

11. Denied.

12. Denied.

The Defendant denies the remaining allegations beginning "WHEREFORE, PREMISES CONSIDERED."

Respectfully submitted,
[CLIENT'S NAME]

By: /s/Attorney Name
Attorney Name

Attorney Name
Firm Name
Address of Firm Line 1
Address of Firm Line 2
Telephone
Telecopier
Email Address
Attorneys for [Client Name]

CERTIFICATE OF SERVICE

The undersigned counsel does hereby certify that this day a true and correct copy of the foregoing instrument was delivered, via ________, to opposing counsel.

SO CERTIFIED, this the _____ day of ____________, [year].

/s/Attorney Name
Attorney Name

Hearing Cancellation

When a hearing is cancelled or continued, there are certain loose ends that need attention.

- **Notify the Court Administrator.** The Court Administrator should be emailed immediately upon the cancellation of a hearing or trial, particularly if the matter is settled. Early notification gives the court opportunity to schedule other matters.
- **Notify the Client.** Make sure the client understands that he or she does not need to appear.
- **Notify Witnesses.** If witnesses have been subpoenaed or arranged to testify, get them immediate notice of the cancellation. Early notice is particularly important if a witness is traveling a long distance. Remember that this also applies to uncooperative witnesses you may have subpoenaed.
- **Make a Calendar Note.** Make a note on the calendar that the hearing is cancelled. If you are using a computer calendar, shrink the time down to just a half an hour and make a note on the calendar entry that the hearing is cancelled. If the hearing is set for another date, make a note on the calendar entry for the old date as to what the new date is. Making such notes makes the calendar tell the story.
- **Prepare an Order.** If the matter is postponed to a later date, draft an agreed order continuing the matter to the new date. If a motion is cancelled due to resolution of the issue, prepare an agreed order or file a notice of the resolution. This keeps the record straight. If the matter is cancelled because the case is settled, then there is no need for an order.

Sending Large Files

Attorneys get a lot of emails, so the last thing you want to do is compound this problem by sending documents via multiple emails because the files are too large to send together as one email.

Mail server restrictions limit not only the size of attachments you can send via email, but also the size of attachments you can receive. This means that even though you may be successful in sending that email with multiple attachments, there is a chance that it may not be received because not all email clients are the same. Save yourself the trouble and invest in programs that are made to send large files—like Dropbox or Adobe Document Cloud.

Dropbox is a useful tool when you need to send multiple documents via one email, and the cost of this subscription is currently $16.58/month for an individual professional. Dropbox may be accessed from any web browser or by downloading the Dropbox application to your computer. Using the Dropbox application, you can easily select the documents you wish to send, right click, and choose the "send a copy" option next to the blue Dropbox symbol:

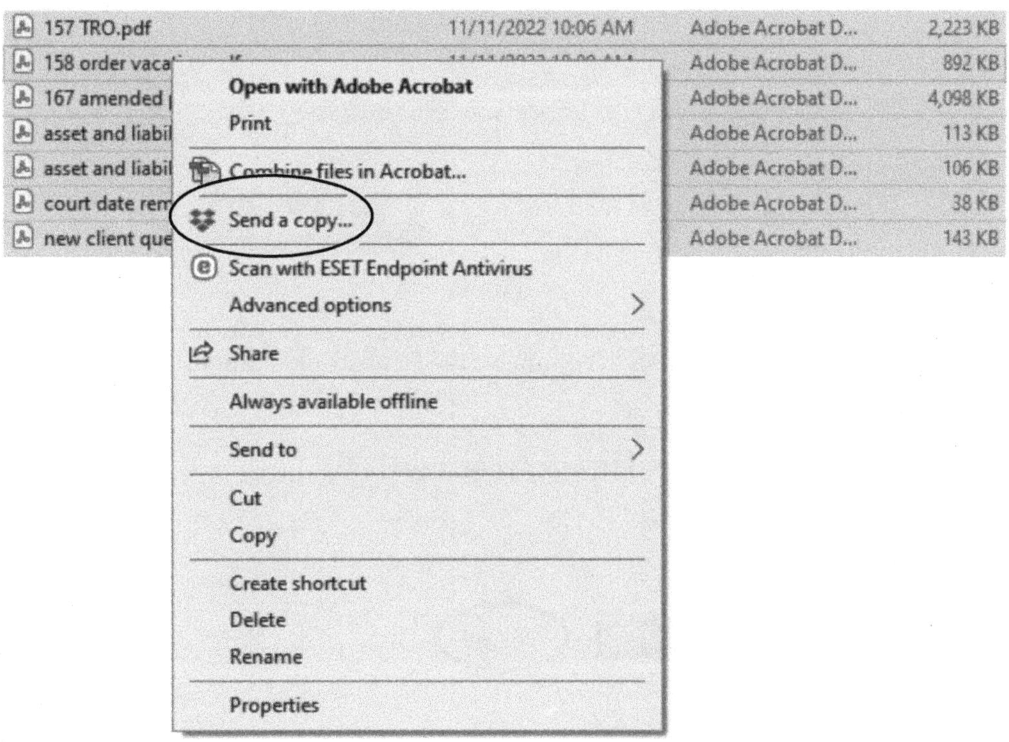

Next, you will be able to review the files you have selected and add more files. Once you are satisfied that you have selected all documents, you simply hit "Create transfer":

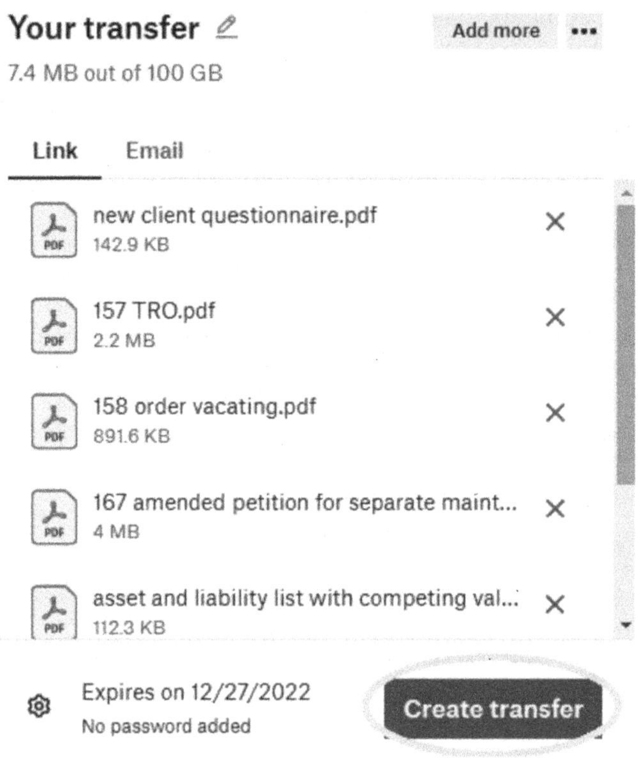

You will have two options to send your documents after you hit "Create transfer"—via email or a link. I highly recommend the "Copy link" option:

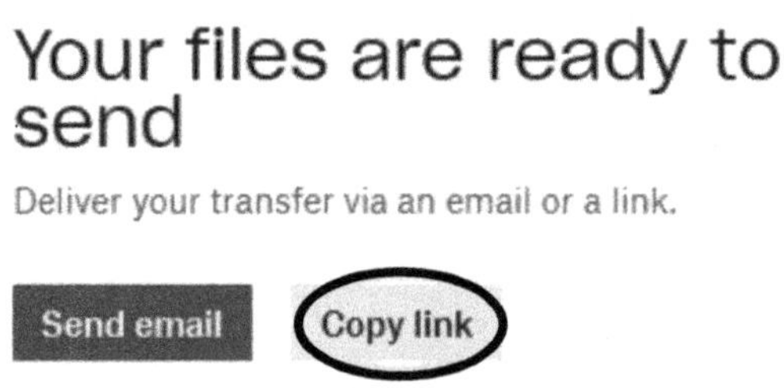

Using the link function, you can still draft your email like you normally would when sending documents. The only difference is you copy and paste the link generated by Dropbox (anyone who receives the link can access the documents) within your email instead of manually attaching individual files. The person on the receiving end of your Dropbox link will then be able to "Download all" documents after clicking the link:

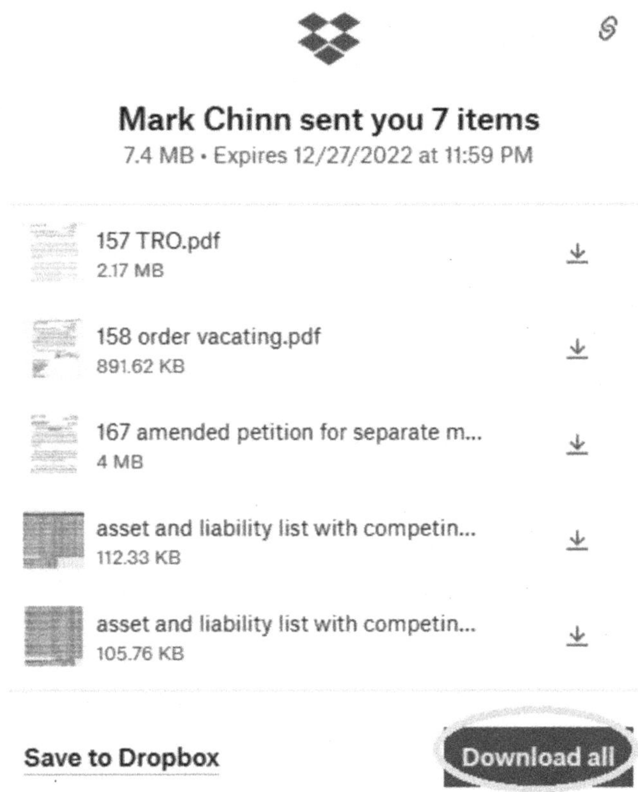

Dropbox is great when you are sending multiple files, but sometimes you just need to send one large document (like four hundred pages of bank statements). An easy way to share single files is through Adobe Document Cloud. To send a document this way, open the PDF in Adobe Acrobat and click the "Share a link to this file" option in the upper right corner:

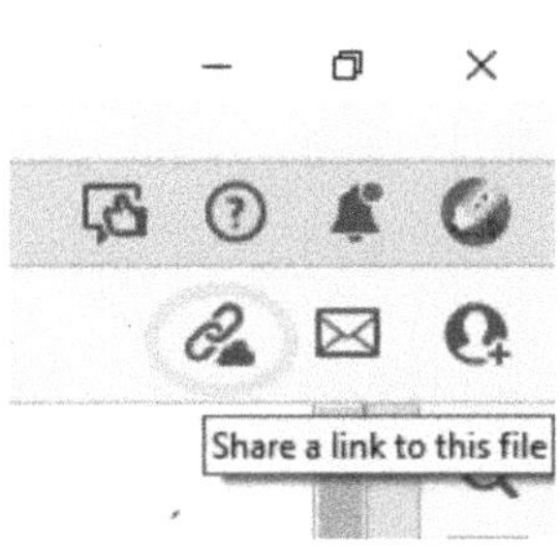

Like Dropbox, Adobe Document Cloud will generate a link that you can copy and paste into your email:

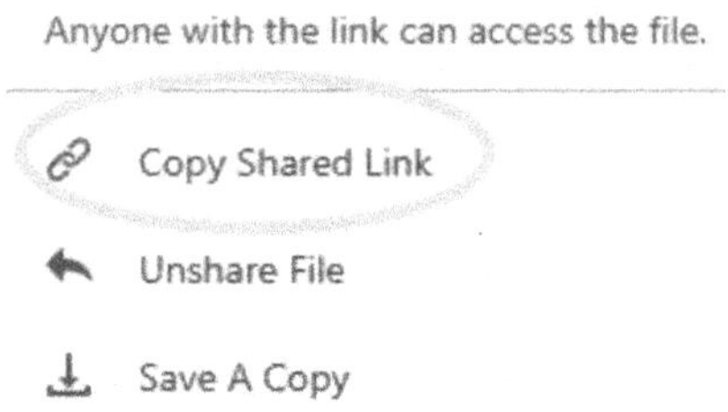

There are other programs you can use to accomplish sending voluminous files besides Dropbox and Adobe Document Cloud, but these are two common file hosting services currently used in law firms. There is not a right way to send large files or multiple documents, but there is a wrong way—sending the documents in multiple emails.

Technology Resources

Lawyers are notorious for resisting new ways of doing things and technology. As a paralegal, you occupy a position where you can help your lawyer improve his or her work by becoming familiar with the different kinds of technologies.

Case Management Software

1. *What Is Case Management Software?*

Case management software provides one central location to track and store client data, schedule contact management, and make case notes, appointment scheduling and history, and client communications, among many other functions.

2. *How Does Case Management Software Work?*

The main functions of case management software are:

- **Intake.** Digital intake forms can capture necessary data in a matter of minutes.
- **Case Management.** Provides tools to record notes, answer service requests, flag issues, send and receive emails, and set reminders.
- **Contact Management.** Keep track of all the persons with whom you come in contact: judges, court administrators, experts, lawyers, referral sources, witnesses, etc. This information is saved in each file so contacts are readily accessible.
- **Referral Source Management.** Keep track of the people who refer you each case and set reminders to stay in touch with them.
- **Document Assembly.** Document assembly software usually accompanies the software and allows for documents that are generated to be saved within the file for easy access.
- **Calendaring.** Create templates for reminder systems for each aspect of the case to increase reliability of preparation staging.
- **Time Keeping.** Most actions will be automatically timed and saved for billing, such as phone calls, appointments, and time spent preparing documents. Time sheets can be eliminated!

3. *Why Is Case Management Software Important?*

- **Increase Productivity.** Staff can log activities, make notes, delegate tasks, and schedule events within the same intuitive interface.
- **Create Reports.** Client progress reports can be tracked and displayed using the reporting tools.

- **Collaborate between Caseworkers.** Information in the management system is automatically made accessible to employees working on a case, allowing for increased accountability and effective collaboration between different teams or departments.
- **Deadline Management and Calendaring.** The biggest nightmare for attorneys is deadlines. Case management software allows for the proper calendaring of deadlines with appropriate reminders.

Some case management software listed on the ABA Technology website are:

- Abacuslaw
- Amicus Attorney
- PCLaw
- PROLaw Ready
- STI PracticeMaster
- Time Matters
- Clio
- Practice Panther
- My Case

Document Assembly

Document assembly functions often accompany case management software. There are also programs dedicated to document assembly. Document assembly software helps you create model templates, answer a few questions to merge into the model templates, and save the pertinent answers for each case in the system. Documents that would take hours to create without the software can be created in minutes. Documents created with assembly software are error free compared to the old "cut and paste" method. Some of the programs are:

- AIA Contract Documents
- Blumberg Excelsior
- Contract Express
- D3—Dynamic Document Drafting by Microsystems
- DealBuilder by Business Integrity
- DirectLaw
- DL Drafting Libraries document assembly
- Exari
- HotDocs

Voice Recognition

For many, many years, lawyers have used dictation to prepare documents.

Many lawyers do not know how to type efficiently and do not wish to prepare documents. Voice recognition software has advanced to the point where it is really effective. The lawyer can see the dictation as she or he dictates. The lawyer can use this for emails or preparation of documents. Here is a list of voice recognition software found on Capterra, a free website helping businesses choose better software.

- LylySpeech
- SpeakEZ
- CallHippo
- Twilio
- Dragon Professional Individual
- Descript
- Sonix
- Transkriptor

When the Attorney Is Away

The absence of an attorney should not create any gap in service. You need to know exactly how your attorney wants things handled when he or she is away. This prevents staff from taking incorrect actions in the absence of a lawyer.

Make sure you sit down with your attorney and develop a protocol for handling business while she or he is away. Here are some key points.

1. *Production Meetings.* Get in the habit of having regular meetings with the attorney and support staff to discuss cases and management of the office. A good time to have this meeting is every Monday morning at 10:30 for about an hour. The agenda for the meeting should be as follows:
    a. Discuss whether there are trials, motions, depositions, or special needs or events to take place during the day.
    b. Discuss any issues presented by the cases or clients.
    c. Discuss any staffing or supply issues.
2. *Financial Matters.* Make sure you understand how the attorney wants money handled. Know your authority to write checks for expenses, such as filing fees. A good rule is that no money is to be returned to a client and no funds are to be paid out of trust (with the exception of standard billing) without express permission of the absent attorney. No one should accept cash from a client without providing a receipt and keeping a copy. Under no circumstances shall more than $10,000 in cash be received from a client. Team members must understand that the bookkeeper may not be present all days of the week; therefore, the requests for funds, such as filing fees, must be anticipated in advance.
3. *Return of Files.* You should be familiar with how to handle a request from a client to return a file. No original document should be given to a client without receiving a receipt from the client.
4. *Family Emergency.* In the event a member of the team needs to contact a member of a lawyer's family, the following rules apply:

    First contact:

    Second contact:

    Other contacts:

    Neighbor:
5. *Monitor Events.* You should be familiar with your attorney's calendar and check the absent attorney's calendar on a daily basis. Also, email should either be placed on autoreply or monitored daily. You should carefully read the daily mail for the firm in general and the absent attorney in particular to determine if anything needs to be done in his or her absence or if any communication needs be made.

Part 3

Document Preparation

Correspondence

Double-check the following items before placing a letter in the mail:

1. Is the letter addressed to the correct person?
2. Are names spelled correctly?
3. Is the reference proper?
4. Are spelling and grammar checked?
5. Is the correct person listed as the sender?
6. Are enclosures included?
7. Is the client copied?
8. Has a copy been retained for the file?

Drafting Pleadings

Drafting pleadings has to be one of the top three roles of the paralegal. The best paralegal is able to complete a pleading subject to a final review by the attorney. Errors in pleadings are embarrassing, if not costly. Here are some tips on drafting pleadings.

- **Document Assembly Software.** The best tool for drafting pleadings is a solid stable of form templates in a document assembly program. Many case management software systems contain document assembly. In addition, there are independent document assembly software, such as HotDocs, that allow for rapid assembly. Once a reliable template is developed, errors can be almost completely erased. So, if your firm does not have document assembly software, do some research and take the idea to your lawyer. It's worth it!
- **Cut and Paste.** The best way to draft a document for your attorney when you do not have document assembly is to search the system for a similar form previously drafted by your attorney. Once you find it, ask your attorney if she or he would like you to use that form as a template. Then begin the "cut and paste" process. Cut and paste can work well, but it leads to several areas of possible error, such as not changing the civil action number, leaving another party's name in a spot, leaving the wrong date of marriage, etc.
- **Use a Checklist.** No matter what system you use, use a checklist to make sure you have completed the pleading properly. Following is a sample.

Practice Tip. Always justify your paragraphs so they have a nice look on the right edge.

Pleadings Error Checklist

- ☐ Is suit in proper county?
- ☐ Is suit in proper court?
- ☐ Are names of parties correctly spelled?
- ☐ Are there page numbers?
- ☐ Has pleading been spell checked?
- ☐ Is there a line for attorney signature?
- ☐ Is there a firm block?
- ☐ Is a signature line for client required? (Note: Clients must sign Divorce, Contempt, and Modification Complaints and Answers to Interrogatories.)
- ☐ Is an oath required?
- ☐ Are exhibits attached?
- ☐ Is there a Certificate of Service?
- ☐ Are correct attorneys on Certificate?
- ☐ If an order, is there a line that says, "SO ORDERED, this the ____ day of __________, [year]"?
- ☐ If an order, does it have approval lines for attorneys?

Preparation of Financial Statements

By Melissa J. Avery, Indianapolis, IN

Financial declarations are generally required by state or local statute or rule. The form generally covers everything from income and expenses to assets and liabilities. It may seem quite overwhelming to clients to complete this form, so some words of guidance from a qualified paralegal will help them to tackle the process and see the value of exchanging this information early in the case. The financial declaration form will provide both sides with a general summary or snapshot of the financial situation of the parties that can be verified later through discovery. Because the discovery process can take many months, it may be the only financial information available to the parties, or the judge, when making decisions on provisional matters.

It can also reveal the need to take action to preserve certain assets or to prevent the dissipation of others. Remind clients that they will be signing this declaration or affidavit under oath and under penalty of perjury. Assure the client that the attorney will review the draft that you are preparing with the client before sending it on to the other side or filing it with the court.

Tips for Preparing Financial Declarations

1. Gather as many documents as possible when preparing the document. The estimates placed on the declaration now will be compared to the documents produced later in discovery, so they need to line up as closely as possible.
2. Train your clients on how to send documents.
   a. No photos or screenshots
   b. Scans or downloads
   c. Full documents with all pages included
3. Pay attention to whether the numbers requested for income and expenses are weekly, monthly, or something else. This can cause a huge difference in the numbers provided. It may not be consistent across the entirety of the form.
4. Alert your attorney to clients with inconsistent income such as bonuses, commissions, overtime, etc.
5. If the client is proposing to move after a provisional hearing, consider preparing two lists of expenses (one in the current residence and one in the proposed new residence).
6. If you don't know the value of an asset such as a piece of real estate or personal property, put a question mark so the client is not getting fenced into a particular number.
7. Do not allow your client to include full account numbers or other personal identifying information.
8. Consider exchanging affidavits instead of filing them with the court.
9. Be prepared to update financial affidavits as the case progresses.

Tips for Preparing the Budget Section

1. When listing expenses, be clear as to whose expenses are included in the budget being provided.
2. Use the client's pay stub to verify taxes withheld from pay as well as other deductions such as health insurance premiums or voluntary retirement contributions.
3. Have the client research annual expenditures and divide by 12 for monthly numbers (or 52 for weekly numbers) to determine an accurate average expense. Example: utilities or childcare expenses.
4. Compare the budget to the client's income, and/or spouse's income, to determine if the numbers make sense and support the theory of your case.

Initial Documents Needed from Client with Child(ren)

This is a sample of what to send the client to prepare her or his financial statement. Certain documents we request, such as bank statements and tax returns, will contain account numbers, Social Security numbers, or other sensitive information. **As a safeguard, please blacken all but the last four numbers of any personal account number or Social Security number printed on the documents you send us.** Otherwise, we will need to redact these documents for you at our regular billing rate.

COMPLETE STATEMENTS ARE REQUIRED whenever requested in the following. (NO screen snapshots or account activity listings.) INCLUDE ALL PAGES.

Income

- Last four pay stubs
- Federal and state tax returns—three most recent years (including W-2s and 1099s, schedules, attachments, and K-1s)
- If self-employed, a copy of the most recent profit and loss statement and copies of CRS-1 Gross Receipts tax reporting forms for the past six months

Bank Information

- Provide copies of bank statements and check registers (electronic or otherwise) on each account for the past 12 months (include date account was opened/closed)

Expenses

- Provide copies of statements or bills for the past six months (electric, gas, phone, trash, water, cell phone, cable, security, rent, mortgage payment, rental contract, etc.)

Child(ren)-Related Expenses

Provide copies of statements or bills for the past 12 months of the following expenses related to your child(ren):

- Health insurance
- Dental insurance
- Counseling expenses
- Any other extraordinary medical or counseling expenses
- School tuition
- Daycare expenses
- After-school care expenses
- Summer camp tuition
- Required school fees/expenses (agenda, lab, uniform, etc.)

Debts

- Provide statements for all credit card bills for the last 12 months
- Provide copies of any loan documents including most recent statement, current balance, payment amount, and due dates
- Provide copies of any other debts indicating the source of debt, balance due, payment amount, and due date

Financial Information

- Provide copies of each financial statement you have issued in the past five years, including loan applications and credit reports

Real Estate

- Provide copies of deeds, mortgages, real estate contracts, lease, closing statements, etc.
- Provide copies of appraisals, comparative market analysis, purchase offers, or other valuations for any personal property, business property, or business interest

Estate Plans, Will, or Trusts

- Provide copies of each document

Vehicles

- Provide copies of titles, registration certificates, and loan documents
- Provide listing from Kelley Blue Book or other support of value including current mileage

Investments

- Provide certificate(s) or statements for each investment account for the past 12 months

Business

- Provide the following documents from all businesses in which you have an interest:
  a. Articles of incorporation and bylaws
  b. Annual financial statements for each of the last three years
  c. Monthly balance sheets for the last 12 months
  d. Monthly profit and loss statements for the last 12 months
  e. Accounts receivable for the last three years
  f. Buy-sell or stock restriction agreements of owner/shareholder
  g. Valuation documents
  h. Business tax returns for the last three years
- If QuickBooks is used, provide a QuickBooks backup for all businesses owned (or co-owned) in .qbb file format, including the QuickBooks version and year, username, and password.

Retirement and Other Benefits

- Most recent retirement summary plan description
- Most recent benefit statement for each plan including retirement, profit sharing, deferred compensation, disability, or pension plans

Checklist: Supporting Financial Documents and Related Information

- *Tax Returns.* If you are able, please furnish us with copies of your state and federal income tax returns for the last five (5) years including all schedules, W-2 forms, and 1099s.
- *Net Worth Statements.* If you or your spouse has been required to file any financial or net worth statements in the last five (5) years for the purposes of securing a loan or line of credit, please furnish us with copies of such financial or net worth statements. If you do not have a copy in your possession, contact the financial institution to which you submitted these statements and obtain copies from it.
- *Retirement Plan.* If you or your spouse is a participant in any profit sharing, pension, Keogh, annuity, or retirement plan from an employer or any prior or concurrent employer, please contact the bookkeeper, plan administrator, or person responsible for the maintenance of such program and request from him or her a copy of the summary plan description, a statement as to the current interest in such plan, and its monetary value. If for any reason you encounter difficulties in obtaining information from your spouse's employer, please contact our office and we will pursue this matter for you.
- *Retirement Accounts.* If you or your spouse is the owner of any individual retirement accounts (IRAs), please provide us with the name of the financial institution, account number, beneficiary, and statement as of the date of filing indicating the balance in the account. Please continue to provide us with any statements you receive while the case is pending.
- *Real Estate—Legal Description.* If you or your spouse has an interest in any real estate, list the address of each such parcel and secure a copy of the legal description for each parcel of real estate. It is important that we have a complete legal description for each parcel of real estate since it will be involved in this particular proceeding and later will be included in pertinent legal documents. If you do not personally have such legal description, you may contact the lending institution that has a financial interest in the parcel of real estate, and they will furnish you with the legal description. The legal description appears in the deed, mortgage, title insurance policy, or abstract of title. Please provide us with a copy of the deed by which you or your spouse took title to the property.
- *Real Estate Appraisal.* If any property has been appraised for any reason within the last three (3) years, such as for insurance, mortgage loan, or contemplation of sale, please furnish us with a copy of the appraisal or the name, address, and phone number of the person who made the appraisal for you.
- *Mortgage.* Please provide the current and previous year end statement regarding the mortgage balance owing on any real estate you or your spouse has an interest in. Be sure to include mortgage company name, address, and telephone number and the account number of your loan.

- *Life Insurance.* You will be requested to furnish us with information concerning all life insurance policies. It is important for us to receive a copy of the fact sheet of all life insurance policies owned setting forth the name of the insurance company, face amount of the policy, policy number, owner of the policy, beneficiary, annual premium, and the terms and conditions of such policy. Also please provide the loans, if any, on the policy.
- *Medical Insurance.* Furnish us with the company name, address, policy or group number, and subscriber number for all health and medical insurance. Also secure from the insurance company a statement as to coverage for the spouse and children and what provision the policy has concerning conversion after divorce.
- *Burial Plots.* If you or your spouse own any burial plots, please provide a copy of the deed(s) to said burial plots.
- *Bank Accounts.* It is important for us to receive the statement as of the date of filing indicating the balance on deposit in all bank, savings and loan, or other financial institution accounts, and we must also receive the account number of each such account. Such information can be obtained by you upon request from the financial institution.
- *Securities.* If you or your spouse owns any securities, please furnish us with a list of the stocks or bonds owned, the date of purchase, the purchase price, and the current owner of such securities. This information can be obtained directly from the person who handled the purchase of these securities for you or your spouse. Please provide us with the monthly or quarterly statement for the date we file and continue to provide the statements when you get them while the case is pending.
- *Business Interests.* If you or your spouse has any interest in any business entity, we must receive copies of such partnership or corporate tax returns and the appropriate schedules attached to such returns, as well as copies of the balance sheets and profit and loss statements, for the last three (3) years. You might find this difficult to obtain if you are not the spouse who has such controlling interest. Please advise us if you encounter difficulties and we will contact the necessary individuals to secure such information.
- *Estate or Trust Interests.* It is also important that you tell us if you or your spouse has any interest in any estate, inheritance, or a future interest that you believe will become your property, or your spouse's property, in the near future. If such is the case, please furnish us with a copy of the will, inventory, final account, and judgment affecting such interest. If you have an interest in any trust, it is important for us to review the actual trust agreement, the inventory, most recent annual account statement, and tax returns, if any, for such trust. We would suggest that you provide us with such documentation for the last five (5) years. Please be sure to furnish us with whatever information you have with respect to your spouse's interest in any estate, trust, or future interests.
- *Previous Marriage.* If either you or your spouse was previously married and divorced, furnish us with copies of the Findings of Fact, Conclusions of Law, and Judgment (Settlement Agreement and Decree) entered in the action.

- *Written Agreements.* If you and your spouse have entered into any written agreement concerning support, property, or other matters, furnish us with a copy of the agreement. If there is no agreement, under no circumstances should you enter into any agreement with respect to these proceedings or otherwise without consultation with this office.
- *Hearing for Temporary Relief.* If we are unable to reach an agreement for temporary support and maintenance during the pendency of the action for yourself and your spouse and your children, you will be required to attend a hearing held before a judge. At the temporary hearing, you will be required to furnish a wage statement from your employer for a period of eight weeks prior to the hearing, setting forth your actual gross and net earnings. You will also be required to produce copies of your income tax returns for at least the last two (2) years. We would remind you to have this information available and forwarded to us in advance of the hearing so that we can properly represent your interests and also be able to properly estimate your needs during such period.
- *Safe Deposit Box.* If you or your spouse has a safe deposit box, please indicate the location and furnish us with a list of the contents.
- *History of Marriage.* Please provide us with a history of the marriage in narrative form. It should include the events leading up to the marriage, what each of you wished out of the marriage, the property each of you brought into the marriage, the jobs and positions held, if either of you changed or altered plans for the other, the help either or both of your families gave to you and your spouse, and the problems of the marriage. This chronology should also trace residences, financial growth and planning, how you accumulated your present property, bad acts by you or your spouse, and short- and long-term goals of you and your spouse.
- *Statement of Expenses.* Please complete the Financial Declaration included in your intake packet given to you at your initial interview and return it to our office.
- *Monthly Trade Credits/Statement of Account.* It will be very helpful to have the actual monthly statement of account from all of your debts for the last twelve (12) months with emphasis on the statement closest to the filing date. In any event, secure as many from each as you are able (Mastercard, Visa, Discover, American Express, Sears, L.S. Ayres, oil company charges, furniture stores, department stores, appliance stores, etc.).
- *Credit Report.* If you are unfamiliar with your debts, you could get your credit report from one or all of the credit bureaus to assist you.
- *Cryptocurrency.* Please provide files downloaded from or exported from the software, website, or institution providing the wallet or exchange containing all transaction histories such as buying, selling, deposits (receipts), withdrawals (sends), conversions to other cryptocurrency, and claims of cryptocurrency forks as well as a screenshot of the beginning and ending balance for each identified account.

Divorce Agreement Completion Checklist

Agreement Completion Checklist. This spreadsheet is designed to identify the closing details of an agreement, assign responsibility, and check off on completion.

File-Closing Checklist

Task	Assigned To	Due Date	Date Complete
1. Enter Divorce			
2. QDRO			
3. IRA Rollover			
4. Prepare Deeds			
5. Auto Title Transfer			
6. Bank Accounts			
7. Stock Transfers			
8. Payment of Money			
9. Payoff of Loan			
10. Transfer of Property			
11. Health Insurance			
12. Auto Insurance			
13. Life Insurance			
14. Disability Insurance			
15. Change Will			
16. Child Dependent Exemption			

Drafting a Divorce Agreement

This is a simple checklist for the drafters of agreements to make sure everything is covered. This checklist may also be given to clients to assist the attorney in drafting or in negotiating with opposing counsel.

Divorce Agreement Checklist

1. Custody
   - Legal
   - Physical
   - Special Provisions
2. Visitation
   - Standard
   - Special Provisions
3. Support
   - Cash
   - Escalation
   - Day Care
   - Special Provisions (Allowance, Cars, Car Insurance and Tags, Clothes)
4. Private School
   - Tuition, Fees
   - Re-enrollment Fees
   - Activity Fees
   - Books
5. Health Insurance
   - Premium
   - Noncovered Medical
   - Definition of Medical
   - Special Provisions
6. College
   - State Supported or Other
   - Division of Responsibility
   - Method of Choosing

- Definition of Expenses
- Special Provisions
- Reduction of Child Support While in Dorm at College

7. Mutual Waiver of Alimony
8. Periodic Alimony
    - Waiver
    - Rehabilitative
    - Bankruptcy Language
9. Lump-Sum Alimony
    - Bankruptcy Language
10. House
    - Exclusive Use
    - Quitclaim or Special Warranty (make sure client is aware that quitclaim of house does not relieve her or him of debt and may interfere with financing another house later)
    - Sale, Terms
    - Personal Possessions Provision
    - Garage Door Openers
    - Security Gate Remote Controls
    - Extra Keys to Car and House
    - Security Codes
    - Utility and Other Deposits
    - Tax and Insurance Escrows
    - Dates to Carry Through Insurance
11. Cars
    - Hers
    - His
    - Provision That Each Retain Respective Car
    - Car License Plate Credits
    - Keys
12. Checking and Savings Accounts
    - Already Split
    - Overdrafts on Joint Checking Accounts

13. Stocks, Bonds
14. Property Division
    - Hotel, Credit Card, and Airline Points
    - Attorney's Fees Paid with Joint Funds
    - Attorney's Fees Trust Fund Balances
15. Businesses
    - Waiver of Interest
16. Pensions
    - Split
    - Waiver
17. Debts
18. Life Insurance
19. Bankruptcy Provision
20. Taxes
    - How to File
    - Dependent Exemptions
    - Innocent Spouse Provision
    - Income Tax Refunds
    - Liability for Improper Preparation or Reporting
    - Liability for Audits
    - Division of Refunds
21. Attorneys
    - Opposing Counsel
    - No Counsel on Other Side
    - Each Pay Respective Fees
22. Release
23. Special Provisions
    - Deed of Trust to Secure Performance
    - Name Change for Wife

Entry of Agreed Divorce

This checklist is designed to make sure the technical details of entering an agreed divorce are covered. Different judges and different counties have different rules. This checklist requires checking into those differences. It is best to get all documents concluded at once. Loose ends are hard to tie up. This checklist prompts the preparation of as many of the closing documents as possible, such as deeds, withholding orders, etc.

Divorce Entry Checklist

CLIENT: ______________________________

1. Date joint complaint filed/defendant served
2. Waiting period days run ______________________________.
3. Agreement prepared
   - Are exhibits attached? (e.g., personal property lists)
   - Are blanks filled in?
   - Notary for both
4. Calendar date to enter judgment
5. County to be entered in
6. Special requirements for that county:
   - Person contacted: ______________________________
7. Does court require specific language in order?
8. Is Qualified Domestic Relations Order necessary?
9. Withholding order?
10. Financial statements. Does the court require exchange of financial statements to be documented in the court file?
11. Other documents:
    - Car titles
    - Deeds
    - Insurance policies
    - Tax documents (e.g., waiver of child exemption)

QDRO Basics

A qualified domestic relations order (QDRO), as defined in 29 U.S.C.S. § 1056, is a domestic relations order that creates or recognizes the existence of an alternate payee's right to receive all or a portion of a participant's benefits under a plan, and the term "domestic relations order" means any judgment, decree, or order (including approval of a property settlement agreement) that relates to the provision of child support, alimony payments, or marital property rights to a spouse, former spouse, child, or other dependent of a participant and is made pursuant to a state domestic relation law. This chapter focuses on QDROs as they relate to property division in a divorce context.

A QDRO is an essential tool in most divorces because it is used to split qualified retirement accounts, like defined contribution plans and defined benefit plans, between spouses without tax consequences. Nonqualified plans are usually not divisible by QDRO and are not subject to the Employee Retirement Income Security Act (ERISA),[1] but there are some exceptions. According to Emily McBurney, Esq., a recognized expert in the field of QDROs, some federal government and military retirement plans are divisible but not subject to ERISA, and dividing these plans should not be attempted without experience or expert advice because these plans are subject to very complex and specific rules.

First, if you are dividing an IRA (individual retirement account), then you do not need a QDRO. A copy of a divorce decree and property settlement agreement plus a letter of instruction or form from the financial institution should suffice to transfer IRA funds from one spouse to another. Some terms and information you will need to know for drafting your QDRO include:

- Participant—This is the spouse whose retirement account is being split. You will need the participant's full address, date of birth, date of participation in the plan you are dividing, employer information, and Social Security number.
- Alternate Payee—This is the former spouse who will be receiving the funds under the QDRO. You will need the alternate payee's full address, date of birth, and Social Security number.
- Plan to Which Order Applies—You must use the correct name of the plan. For example, "Capital One Financial Corporation Associate Savings Plan" is correct, but you should never use "Wife's Retirement Plan" or "Husband's Retirement Plan." You will need a retirement statement from the participant to get this information.
- Valuation Date—This information should be in your property settlement agreement and can be the date of either separation or divorce depending on what date the retirement plan is considered the other party's separate, nonmarital funds. This date is important because it will determine the account's value prior to segregating the funds.

1. The U.S. Department of Labor defines ERISA as a federal law that sets minimum standards for most voluntarily established retirement and health plans in private industry to provide protection for individuals in these plans. In general, ERISA does not cover plans established or maintained by governmental entities, churches for their employees, or plans that are maintained solely to comply with applicable workers compensation, unemployment, or disability laws. https://www.dol.gov/general/topic/retirement/erisa

- Earnings and losses do affect the division of a defined contribution plan. Therefore, the QDRO will need to state whether the alternate payee's award is or is not entitled to earnings (defined as gains, losses, dividends, and interest) from the valuation date to the date that the award is segregated from the participant's account.
- Surviving Spouse Benefits—You must address what happens if the participant dies before the alternate payee receives his or her benefits. For example, "If participant dies before the above-stated amount from the plan has been paid to alternate payee, alternate payee shall be treated as surviving spouse for the amount stated above."
- QDRO Processing Fees—You should check in advance whether the plan will charge an administrative fee and, if so, specify whether this fee will be split by the parties or if one party will be solely responsible.

You should always double-check any QDRO form you use. Sometimes, you can streamline the QDRO process and use online QDRO generating systems. For example, Fidelity has an online QDRO center that allows you to input your data and it will assemble your QDRO. Other times you can use a form like the one at the end of this chapter. You should always try and submit a draft of the QDRO to the plan administrator for review prior to it being signed by the parties and entered by the court just in case the plan administrator rejects the QDRO you drafted.

Never close a file without obtaining some form of certification from the plan administrator that the final QDRO has been received and accepted. This approval letter may be simple and state the QDRO has been received and approved as qualified, but others may be more detailed and set forth the plan administrator's interpretation of your QDRO. Always save these letters and review for any discrepancies between the plan administrator's interpretation of your QDRO and what the QDRO actually says. It is very important to retain a copy of the approval letter so you will have proof that the plan administrator did in fact receive and approve your QDRO if there are any issues later with the alternate payee receiving the funds.

IN THE __________ COURT OF __________ COUNTY, __________
__________ JUDICIAL DISTRICT

[NAME OF PLAINTIFF] **PLAINTIFF**

VS. **CAUSE NO. ______________**

[NAME OF DEFENDANT] **DEFENDANT**

QUALIFIED DOMESTIC RELATIONS ORDER

THIS DAY this cause came on to be heard in connection with and pursuant to the Final Judgment of Divorce filed on [Date of Final Judgment of Divorce], page _____ of _____ in document #_____, and in accordance with said Final Judgment of Divorce, the Court orders the following, to wit:

IT IS ORDERED AND ADJUDGED that, pursuant to said Final Judgment of Divorce filed on [Date of Final Judgment of Divorce], page _____ of _____ in document #_____, the Participant, ___________, shall convey by QDRO [Pension or Retirement Account being conveyed by QDRO] as of the [date of division or valuation date]. This Court hereby orders, pursuant to Title 26 United States Code, Section 414(p), that this Order shall serve as a Qualified Domestic Relations Order (QDRO), as defined thereunder, and that [Alternate Payee's Name] shall be awarded, assigned, and have transferred to [him/her], as Alternate Payee, direct from Participant's [Plan to which order applies] account as follows:

1. **Plan to Which Order Applies.** [Plan to Which Order Applies]
2. **Administrator.** [Name of Plan Administrator]
3. **Employer.** [Employer's Name]
4. **Administrator's Telephone Number.** [Administrator's Telephone Number]
5. **Participant and Sponsor.** [Participant's Full Name]
6. **Participant's Last Known Mailing Address.** [Participant's Last Known Mailing Address]
7. **Participant's Social Security #.** xxx-xx-[Last Four of Participant's Social: 9999]
8. **Participant's Date of Birth.** [Participant's Date of Birth: 6/3/1990]
9. **Participant's Date of Participation.** [Participant's Date of Participation]
10. **Alternate Payee.** [Name of Person Receiving Benefits]
11. **Alternate Payee's Mailing Address.** [Alternate Payee's Mailing Address]
12. **Alternate Payee's Social Security #.** xxx-xx-[Last Four of Alternate Payee's Social: 9999]

13. **Alternate Payee's Date of Birth.** [Alternate Payee's Date of Birth: 6/3/1990]

14. **Amount of Participant's Benefit to Be Paid to Alternate Payee.** Alternate Payee, [Name of person receiving benefits], shall be transferred ________________ as of [Valuation Date or Date of Distribution]. The distribution should take place on the earliest date on which a distribution to the Alternate Payee is allowed to occur, in accordance with the Provisions of the Internal Revenue Code. The Plan Administrator shall segregate the aforesaid amount prior to distribution as soon as is practicable. If Participant dies before the above-stated amount from the Plan has been paid to Alternate Payee, Alternate Payee shall be treated as surviving spouse for the amount stated above.

15. **Alternate Payee's Rights.** Alternate Payee has the sole and exclusive right, with respect to [his/her] interest in the Plan, to:

    a) Direct and manage the investment of [his/her] interest provided [his/her] interest has vested as defined in Paragraph 14 above, and Participant shall have no control of [his/her] interest after vesting;

    b) Withdraw [his/her] Plan interest on or after the date the Plan Administrator determines this to be a QDRO and [his/her] interest has vested. The Alternate Payee may elect distribution in any form permitted under the Plan to the Participant; however, the Alternate Payee may not select a joint and survivor annuity with respect to a later spouse.

    This Paragraph 15 applies pending the Plan Administrator's determination of whether or not this order is a QDRO. The Participant must honor the Alternate Payee's written directions on matters set forth in this Paragraph 15 and its subparagraphs with respect to the Alternate Payee's interest in the Plan. The Participant must execute and deliver to the Plan Administrator or other appropriate official written instructions to implement the Alternate Payee's written instructions.

16. **Income Taxes.** Alternate Payee is ordered and decreed to report any retirement payments received on any applicable income tax return. The Administrator is authorized to issue the appropriate Internal Revenue Form for any direct payment made to Alternate Payee.

17. **Constructive Trustee.** While it is anticipated that the Administrator will pay directly to Alternate Payee the benefit awarded to [him/her], Participant is designated a constructive trustee to the extent [he/she] receives any retirement benefits under the Plan that are due to Alternate Payee but paid to Participant. Participant is ordered and decreed to pay the benefit defined herein directly to Alternate Payee within three days after receipt by [him/her].

18. **Commencement of Payment to Alternate Payee.** Subsequent to the administrator's determination that this Order constitutes a QDRO, either as soon as the Alternate Payee notifies the administrator of the account to which payment is to be made, or such later date as elected by Alternate Payee, in accordance with the terms of the Plan or under such terms as Alternate Payee and the Plan Administrator agree. Notwithstanding any other provision hereof,

payment shall be made in the time and manner provided by Section 414(p) of the Internal Revenue Code of 1986.

19. Method of Payment. Lump sum in cash, or such other method as Alternate Payee may elect pursuant to the plan document.

20. Remarriage. Subsequent remarriage of either party shall not affect the disposition described above.

21. Qualified Domestic Relations Order. This QDRO is made pursuant to the laws of the State of ______________ and the Final Judgment of Divorce filed on [Date of Final Judgment of Divorce], page _____ of _____ in document #_____, wherein the marriage of the parties was dissolved. Said Judgment of Divorce is incorporated herein by reference as though the same were fully copied herein. This QDRO relates to the marital property rights of [Person Receiving Benefits] to receive benefits under the plan and is an equitable distribution of marital property under said laws and judgment. In no event shall this QDRO require the plan to a) provide any type or form of benefit or any option not otherwise provided under the Plan, b) require the Plan to provide increased benefits (determined on the basis of actuarial value) not available to the Participant, or c) require the payment of benefits to [Person Receiving Benefits] that are required to be paid to another alternate payee under another order previously determined to be a QDRO. This provision is intended by the parties to fulfill the requirements of a QDRO as defined in Section 414(p) of the Internal Revenue Code of 1986. If modification becomes necessary to qualify this provision as a QDRO, the parties agree to modify this provision without changing the benefits payable to the Alternate Payee. Likewise, the ______ Court of ________ County, _______________, shall retain jurisdiction to amend this provision to the extent necessary to establish or maintain its qualification as a QDRO, provided that no such amendment shall require the plan to provide any type or form of benefit, or any option, not otherwise provided under the plan. The parties hereto confirm and acknowledge that they are unaware of any prior orders that purport to dispose of the benefits described herein.

22. Notice. Copies of this Order shall be forwarded, by first-class, United States mail, by [Alternate Payee's Lawyer OR Participant's Lawyer] to the Plan Administrator, and pursuant to 29 U.S.C. § 1056(d)(3)(G), the Plan Administrator shall:

  a. Promptly notify the Participant, the Alternate Payee, and any other alternate payee of:

    1. The Plan Administrator's receipt of a copy of this order, and

    2. The Plan's procedures for determining the qualified status of domestic relations orders;

  b. Within a reasonable period of time after receipt of a copy of this order, determining whether this order is a QDRO and notify the Court, the Participant, the Alternate Payee, and any other alternate payee of the determination; and,

c. During the period the Plan Administrator is determining the qualified status of this order, segregate, into a separate account in each Plan or into an escrow account, the amounts that would have been payable to the Alternate Payee during such period had this order been determined to have been a QDRO pursuant to 29 U.S.C. § 1056(d)(3)(H)(I). This paragraph applies pending determination of whether or not this order is a QDRO.

SO ORDERED, AND ADJUDGED, this the ____ day of ________, 20xx.

____
CHANCELLOR

APPROVED:

Attorney Name
Firm Name
Address of Firm Line 1
Address of Firm Line 2
Telephone
Telecopier
Email Address
Attorneys for [Client Name]

APPROVED AS TO FORM:

____
[Opposing Counsel]
[Opposing Counsel Firm Name]
ATTORNEYS FOR ________

Part 4

Discovery

Discovery

Discovery may be the most essential element of preparation for either settlement or trial, and it may be the most key role for paralegals. Here are the main types of discovery:

- Interrogatories. Interrogatories are simply questions submitted to the opposing party in written form. Interrogatories should ask about the following categories of information:
    - Witnesses
    - Expert witnesses
    - Documents pertaining to elements of proof
    - Financial information
    - Parties' statement of facts supporting various claims
- **Requests for Documents.** This procedure allows lawyers to force a party to produce documents relevant to the issues of the case. Documents requested normally include financial documents and documents supporting claims to the divorce.
- **Depositions.** This procedure allows lawyers to compel both parties and any other witness to appear and answer questions under oath. The deposition is typically recorded both audibly and stenographically by a court reporter. The witness is sworn in prior to the testimony. A party may attend the deposition of any witness, as well as that of the other party.
- **Subpoenas duces tecum.** This procedure allows a party to make third parties and witnesses produce documents. The subpoena is served upon a third person or entity not a party, and they are typically required to respond within ten days. The subpoenaed party is usually entitled to recover reasonable expenses for producing the documents. Places that are typically subpoenaed are:
    - Banks for financial documents
    - Employers for wage and disciplinary information
    - Schools for grades of children
    - Healthcare professionals for medical or counseling records
    - Law enforcement for criminal records

Best Practices and Tips

- **Have an established standard set.** Work with your attorney to create a "standard" set of discovery that can easily be generated and sent out. This standard set should be as comprehensive as possible so that nothing is left unrequested. The attorney should examine the standard set to add any particular questions relating to the particular issues of the case.
- **Have a policy of immediately issuing discovery.** Have a policy, subject to your attorney's guidance, of sending discovery at the outset of your involvement in the case. For example, if you are serving a complaint, serve discovery with the complaint. If you have received a complaint, issue discovery immediately to the other side. Having these policies will ensure that basic due diligence is done right away. You don't want to be working on a file down the road and realize you have never asked the other side who their witnesses are!
- **Send the opposing party a copy in Word.** Sending the discovery to the opposing party in Word (or WordPerfect) makes it easy for them to respond by placing the question or request first. This is required in some jurisdictions and certainly makes it easier for everyone to follow the questions and answers.
- **Create templates for your subpoenas.** It is guaranteed that whatever you do today, you will do again in the near future. Create templates for each of your subpoenas that ask for what you are going to typically need so all that is required is a final review to make sure you are getting what you want.
- **Be aware of costs and advise the client in advance.** Depositions and subpoenas cost money. Clients will often exhort the attorney to subpoena everything and depose everyone. That is fine, but they should be advised on the front end that depositions cost hundreds of dollars, subpoenas have to be served, and there may be costs for production. A best practice is to get an estimate up front and ask the client if she or he wishes to incur the expense.
- **Contact subpoenaed entities in advance (unless it would be stupid to do so).** After checking with your attorney, contact the entity that you are going to subpoena, such as a bank, and ask about the best way to serve the subpoena or if the subpoenaed entity will accept the subpoena by fax or email, thus saving some client cost. It is also good practice to ask the subpoenaed entity if it can tell you what the response might cost. For example, the client may have asked for five years of checks and statements, but upon talking to the bank, you learn the cost will be $800. This is an occasion when you discuss with your attorney and the client cutting the request down to two or three years, as long as that still gets the real job done.
- **Set appropriate calendar responses for a discovery request.** Once a discovery request is made, set a calendar reminder for the response date, which is usually 30 days, but ten days in the case of subpoenas (in most jurisdictions).

- **Cooperate in setting depositions where possible.** Contact opposing counsel by email suggesting several dates and times for depositions. Give them a couple of days to respond. If there is no cooperation, send an email letting them know you are going to pick a certain date if you do not hear from them. Courtesy is important, and it is also practical because you will avoid motions for continuance and unnecessary conflict. In addition, if you treat them with courtesy, there is a better chance courtesy will come back your way.
- **Confirm the court reporter by email and note the arrangement on the calendar.** More than once, attorneys have gotten down to final preparation for a deposition and realized no one has arranged a court reporter. Arrange with the other side who is going to arrange the reporter and confirm that by email. Once the court reporter is arranged, indicate the method of arrangement on the calendar entry so someone checking the calendar can clearly see it has been arranged.
- **Always include an authentication affidavit.** One of the best tools that lawyers have for trial preparation is the "self-authenticating affidavit" pursuant to Rule of Evidence 902. This rule allows for any subpoenaed document to be authenticated and therefore admissible into evidence if there is an affidavit accompanying the records subpoenaed. In fact, our firm has stopped asking the other party for documents we can get from a dependable third party for several reasons: (1) the response is accurate; there is not going to be a missing statement or page; (2) the documents can be admitted into evidence without any trouble; and (3) the documents are usually provided without trouble.

Deposition Preparation Calendaring

Depositions can sneak up on the attorney, so calendaring preparation is critical. When a deposition is noticed, calendar the following events:

- 30 days out—arrange court reporter and document arrangements in calendar.
- 25 days out—arrange appointment with client to prepare for deposition.
- 20 days out—verify that all documents necessary to take the deposition are in order.
- 10 days out—block out time for attorney to work on questions.
- 5 days out—prepare deposition notebook and create document folders with three copies of all documents the attorney intends to use.
- 1 day out—verify court reporter and finalize deposition notebook and documents.

Uniform Interstate Depositions and Discovery Act (UIDDA)

The Uniform Interstate Depositions and Discovery Act (UIDDA) provides a way for litigants in state court to take depositions and obtain discovery from individuals and entities located out of state. At least 47 states have adopted some form of the UIDDA, so it is recommended to check the chart published by the Uniform Law Commission to see which states have enacted the UIDDA (either by statute or by rule).

One use of the UIDDA in practice is its application to a subpoena duces tecum. For example, you issue a subpoena duces tecum for an opposing party's bank records, but the bank will not honor the subpoena because it does not do business in the state where your action is pending. The solution is the UIDDA. The following is a checklist to guide you through using the UIDDA:

1. Verify that your state and the state in which you are seeking the discovery have each enacted some form of the UIDDA.
2. Draft your subpoena for issuance in your state as you normally would.
3. Read the rule in the foreign jurisdiction regarding issuance of subpoenas and the UIDDA rules that are applicable to that jurisdiction to make sure your subpoena meets all requirements, like the names, addresses, and telephone numbers of all counsel of record in the proceeding and any party not represented by counsel.
4. Find out in which court you need to file your foreign subpoena. For example, it may be the county in which the business entity is located.
5. Call the clerk's office of that court to verify its requirements for issuing foreign subpoenas, including whether it requires a petition and how much the filing fee will be.
6. Using the subpoena you already drafted, incorporate the new case style above your state case and incorporate that state's rule of civil procedure. It is worth Googling filings in the new state court to see how they set out their case styles.
7. File your petition with the filing fee (if required) and request the new subpoena to be issued in the state court where you are seeking the discovery.
8. Serve your issued, foreign subpoena on the business entity you are seeking records from.

NO.____________________

IN RE JAN JONES	**IN THE DISTRICT COURT**
RE PRODUCTION OF RECORDS	**DALLAS COUNTY, TEXAS**
	____JUDICIAL DISTRICT

IN THE CHANCERY COURT OF MADISON COUNTY, MISSISSIPPI

JAN JONES	**PLAINTIFF**
VS.	**CAUSE NO. XXXXXX**
JACK JONES	**DEFENDANT**

PETITION FOR ISSUANCE OF SUBPOENA DUCES TECUM

COMES NOW, [Attorney Name], the Law Firm of [Your Law Firm], [Your Law Firm Address], [Your Law Firm Telephone Number], Attorney for the Petitioner.

TO THE HONORABLE COURT

The above-entitled action is pending in the State of __________, county of _________, case number XXXXXX. Petitioner Jan Jones requests the issuance of a District Court Subpoena Duces Tecum for Records directed to the Custodian of Records of [Name of Financial Institution and Address] and in support of this motion shows:

1. Petitioner is a party in a civil action in the ______ Court of ______ County, ______. Petitioner and Respondent are husband and wife and are involved in divorce proceedings.

2. Applicant needs to subpoena the records of this third-party witness to obtain documents related to marital property that may be divided by this court action.

WHEREFORE, Applicant requests that the court order the clerk of the court to issue a Subpoena Duces Tecum Re Production of Records and Notice to Opposing Counsel that are attached to this motion.

This the _____ day of ____________, [year].

Respectfully submitted,
[CLIENT'S NAME]

By: /s/Attorney Name
Attorney Name

Attorney Name
Firm Name
Address of Firm Line 1
Address of Firm Line 2
Telephone
Telecopier
Email Address
Attorneys for [Client Name]

NO.____________________

IN RE JAN JONES	**IN THE DISTRICT COURT**
RE PRODUCTION OF RECORDS	**DALLAS COUNTY, TEXAS**
	_____JUDICIAL DISTRICT

IN THE CHANCERY COURT OF MADISON COUNTY, MISSISSIPPI

JAN JONES	**PLAINTIFF**
VS.	**CAUSE NO. XXXXXX**
JACK JONES	**DEFENDANT**

SUBPOENA DUCES TECUM

WE COMMAND YOU TO SUMMON:

To: [NAME OF FINANCIAL INSTITUTION]
C/O [NAME OF REGISTERED AGENT IF APPLICABLE]
[FINANCIAL INSTITUTION ADDRESS LINE 1]
[FINANCIAL INSTITUTION ADDRESS LINE 2]

Pursuant to [Foreign Rule of Civil Procedure for Subpoenas], you are to produce the documents listed below by delivering copies of the documents, certified by you to be true and correct copies, to the law offices of [Name and Address of Your Firm], on or before ten days after the date of service.

1. All financial statements for ________ (SS# xxx-xx-[Last Four of Social Security Number]), or any accounts in which ________ has an interest, from [Beginning Date of Requested Info] to present.

2. Checking statements and returned checks for accounts for ________ (SS# xxx-xx-[Last Four of Social Security Number]), or any accounts in which ________ has an interest or is a signatory, from [Beginning Date of Requested Info] through the present.

3. Statements for any and all savings accounts for ________ (SS# xxx-xx-[Last Four of Social Security Number]), or any accounts in which ________ has an interest, from [Beginning Date of Requested Info] through the present.

4. All loan applications or files for loans to ________ (SS# xxx-xx-[Last Four of Social Security Number]), or any accounts in which ________ has an interest, from [Beginning Date of Requested Info] through the present.

5. Documents in your possession regarding any other financial information pertaining to ________ (SS# xxx-xx-[Last Four of Social Security Number]), or any accounts in which ________ has an interest, from [Beginning Date of Requested Info] through the present.

6. Any and all documents evidencing any and all sales of property transactions or loans involving ________ (SS# xxx-xx-[Last Four of Social Security Number]), or any accounts in which ________ has an interest, from [Beginning Date of Requested Info] through the present, including but not limited to all closing documents, loan applications, financial statements, analysis, appraisals, statements, writings, and reports.

You are expected to produce the foregoing documents pursuant to Rule [Foreign Rule of Civil Procedure for Subpoenas] of the [Foreign State] Rules of Civil Procedure without necessity of an appearance by mailing copies of the documents, certified by you to be true and correct copies, to [Name and Address of Your Firm], on or before the date indicated.

IF WE CAN OBTAIN COPIES OF THESE DOCUMENTS THAT RESPOND TO THIS SUBPOENA, YOUR APPEARANCE WILL NOT BE NECESSARY. PLEASE PROVIDE US WITH AN INVOICE FOR ALL COPY CHARGES.

FAILURE BY ANY PERSON WITHOUT ADEQUATE EXCUSE TO OBEY A SUBPOENA SERVED UPON THAT PERSON MAY BE DEEMED IN CONTEMPT OF THE COURT FROM WHICH THE SUBPOENA IS ISSUED OR A DISTRICT COURT IN THE COUNTY IN WHICH THE SUBPOENA IS SERVED, AND MAY BE PUNISHED BY FINE OR CONFINEMENT, OR BOTH.

You are not required to file an answer or other pleading, but you may do so if you desire.

WITNESS MY SIGNATURE and seal of office, this the _____ day of __________, [year].

________________, Clerk
District Court Clerk

BY: ________________________D.C.

Attorney Name
Firm Name
Address of Firm Line 1
Address of Firm Line 2
Telephone
Telecopier
Email Address
Attorneys for [Client Name]

CERTIFICATE OF SERVICE

The undersigned counsel does hereby certify that this day a true and correct copy of the foregoing instrument was delivered, via ________, to opposing counsel:

[Name of Opposing Counsel]
[Address of Opposing Counsel]
[Phone Number of Opposing Counsel]

SO CERTIFIED, this the _____ day of ____________, [year].

/s/Attorney Name
Attorney Name

Bates Numbering Documents

Bates numbering, also known as Bates stamping, is a method of sequentially numbering pages and is commonly used in the legal profession, the business profession, and the medical field. Bates numbering your documents in the legal profession is essential to the discovery phase and the trial. In discovery, you will need a system to catalogue every single document (could be thousands) that you are producing to the other side including the date it was sent. At trial, the attorney will need Bates numbered pages to help identify each document being offered as an exhibit. Think of Bates numbering as page numbers—starting with the first page of your first document and ending with the last page of the last document you send to opposing counsel throughout the litigation. It is essential to always number your documents for each case in sequence without starting back at 1. It will not help you to log and track your documents if multiple documents are Bates numbered as 000001.

Bates Numbering Your Documents

Adobe Acrobat Pro is a tool that most attorneys already have, and it can be used to easily add Bates numbers to your documents. To use this function, start by opening the document you want to number in Adobe Acrobat Pro and select the "stamp" symbol from your Adobe Acrobat tools pane:

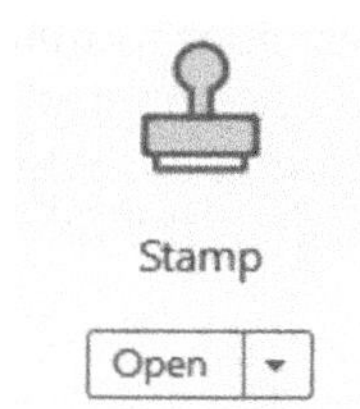

You will then be prompted with the following options:

After selecting "Bates Numbering" and then "Add," you will select "Output Options" at the bottom of the screen:

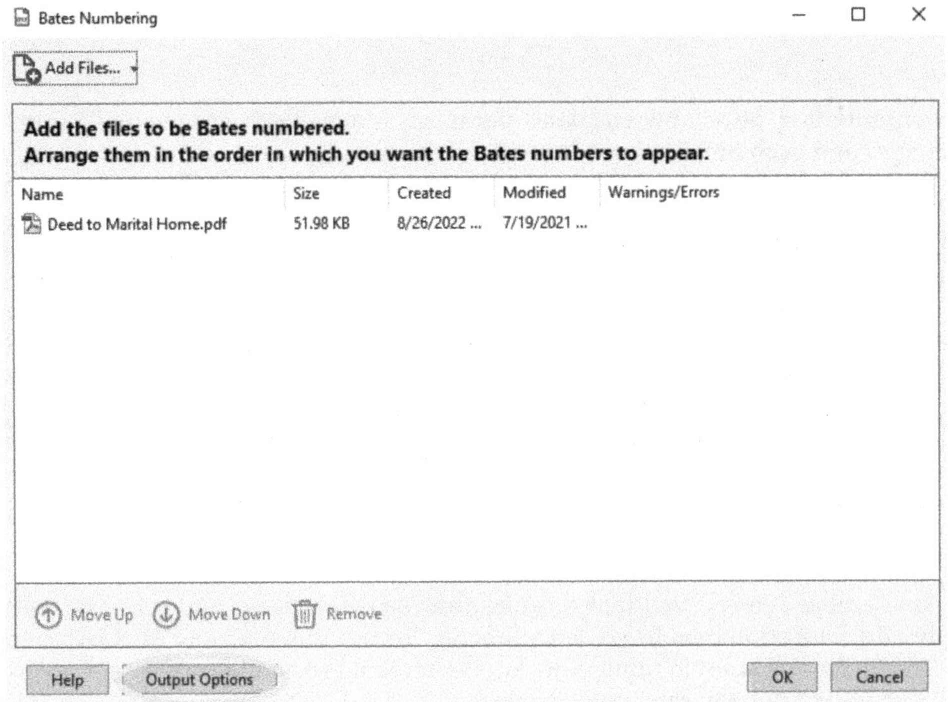

The output options are a necessary step to making your Bates numbering system usable. By selecting "Add to original file names" and typing the prompt %BATES_NUMBER_KEY% in the "Insert Before" box, your finished product will have Bates numbers not only on the page but also in the title of your document for easy searchability later:

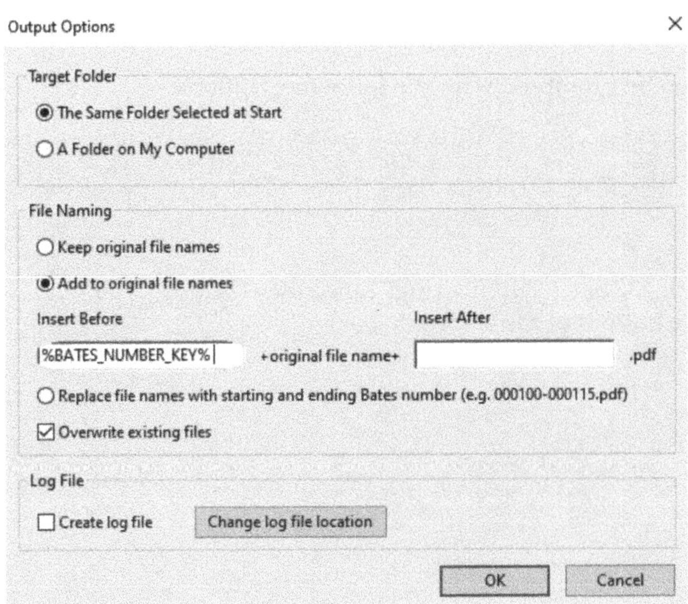

Next, select "OK" and you will be returned to the previous screen where you will select "OK" again. You will then be directed to a screen called "Add Header and Footer" where you will add the Bates number and date:

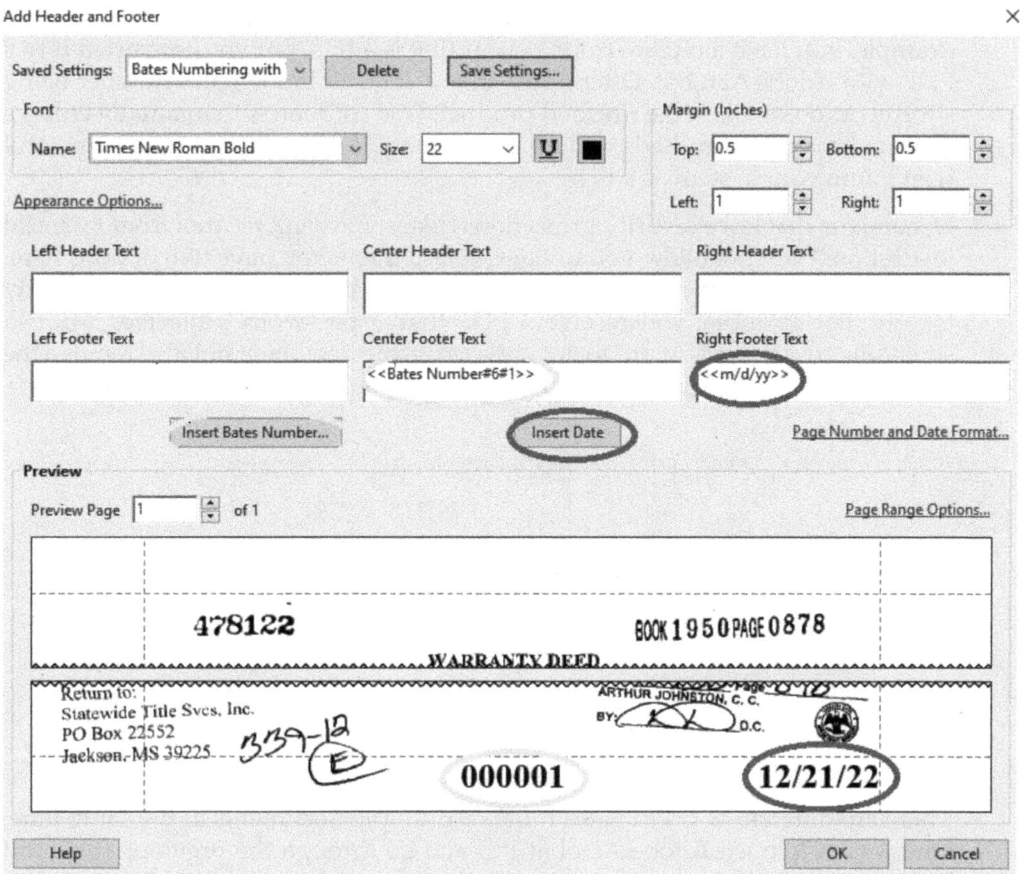

Your settings may not be the same for each document, but you should try to find a font, size, and margin size that generally work for your firm and save that setting for future documents. Some tips when Bates numbering documents:

- Title your document properly before adding Bates numbers.
- Always hit the space bar after typing %BATES_NUMBER_KEY% to ensure that there is a space between the number of your document and the title of the document:

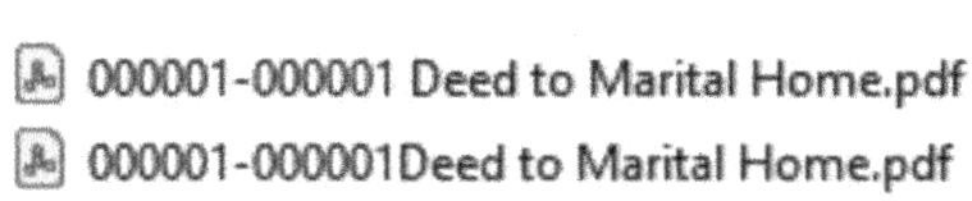

- Do not stamp over other words on the page.
- Make sure the number and date are large enough for everyone to read.

- Stamp the date you are actually sending the document to opposing counsel.
- Do not stamp documents unless you are ready to log them and send them to opposing counsel.
- Be careful stamping documents that were originally in a picture format. For example, you have a picture from a client that is a JPG, but you converted it to a PDF with Adobe Acrobat. Oftentimes, this will result in the Bates number being shrunk or too small on the finished product. One solution is to manually enlarge the number on the finished product. Another solution is to print the picture and scan it into your system as a PDF.
- Documents that have security protections (like some bank records from financial institutions) will not allow you to Bates stamp them. You have two options here. You can either print the documents and scan them back in or remove the security feature. For example, you receive a PDF that is password protected. You can sometimes use this password to not only access the document but also remove the security feature stopping you from numbering your document under "Protect":

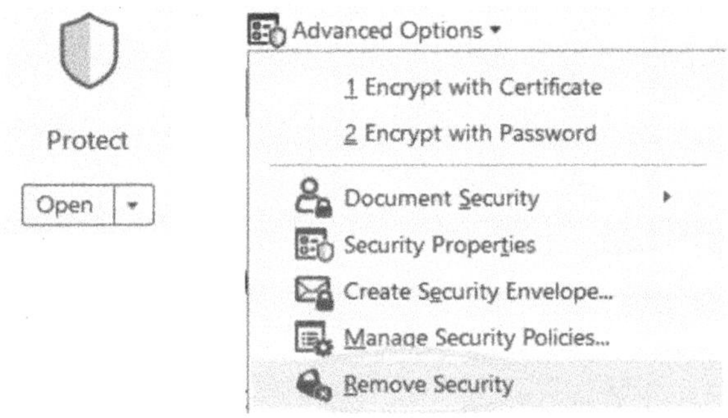

- There are different ways to Bates number multiple documents at the same time. One way is to open Adobe Acrobat Pro and go through the previous steps (hit Tools > Bates Numbering > Add) and use the "Add files . . ." option to select entire folders of documents:

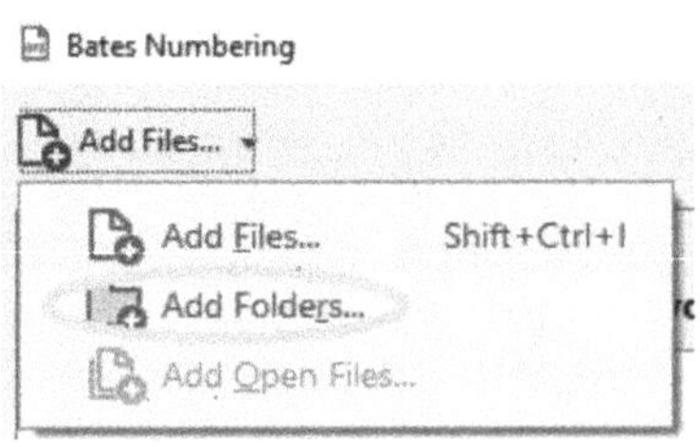

- Another option is to open every document you want to Bates number, but this time you will select "Add Open Files" instead of "Add Folders":

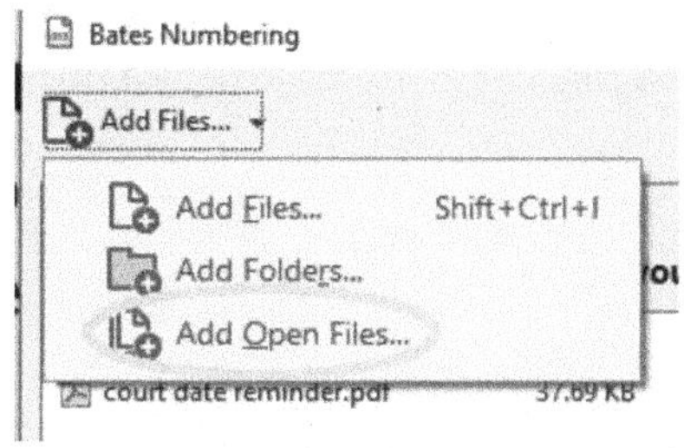

Creating a Bates Numbers Log

You should create a Bates numbers log each and every time you stamp documents to easily keep track of every document you send and when you sent it. If Adobe Acrobat will not create a file log for you, the backup option is to use Excel to copy and paste your numbered documents into a Word document. To do so, first highlight all of your documents and hit "Copy Path":

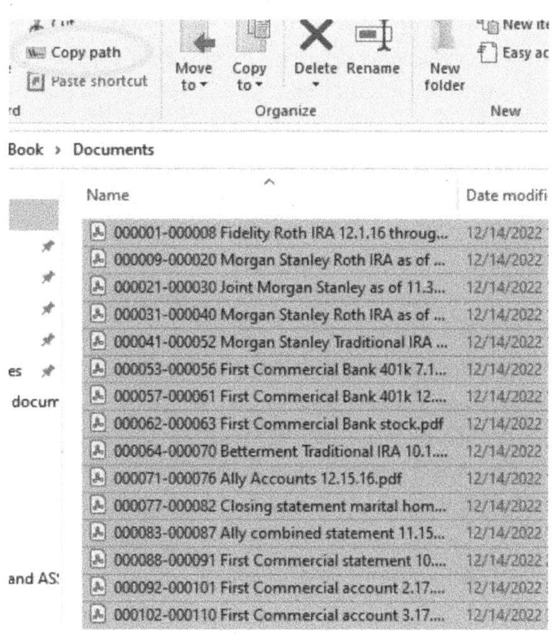

Open a blank workbook in Excel followed by "Paste" or use the shortcut "Control-V." Once you have pasted your document names into Excel, you will need to remove the file path in front of each number. This can be done quickly by highlighting everything in Excel and using the Find and Replace function (note you will leave "Replace with" blank) followed by "Replace All" to remove the unwanted text:

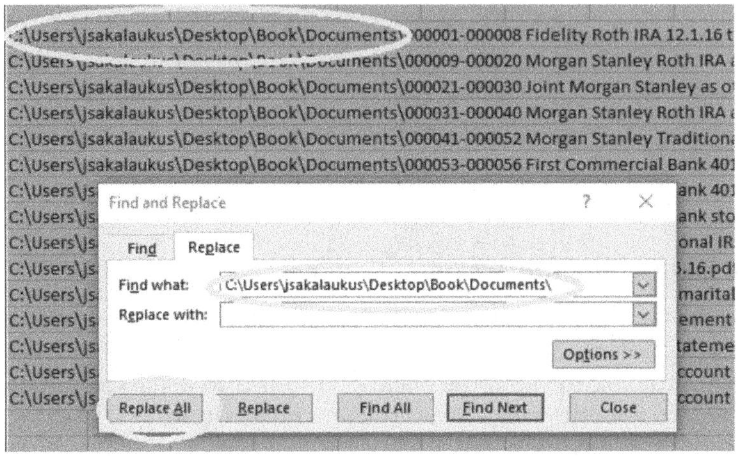

After the file path is removed, you can copy and paste your numbered document list into a Word document. You should only create one log per client, and the title of your log should be the same for each client so it is easily accessible by other members of your office:

BATES LOG

EMAILED 12.21.22:

000001-000008	Fidelity Roth IRA 12.1.16 through 12.31.16.pdf
000009-000020	Morgan Stanley Roth IRA as of 11.30.22.pdf
000021-000030	Joint Morgan Stanley as of 11.30.22.pdf
000031-000040	Morgan Stanley Roth IRA as of 11.30.22.pdf
000041-000052	Morgan Stanley Traditional IRA as of 11.30.22.pdf
000053-000056	First Commercial Bank 401k 7.1.22 through 9.30.22 plan 6701.pdf
000057-000061	First Commercial Bank 401k 12.1.16 through 12.31.16.pdf
000062-000063	First Commercial Bank stock.pdf
000064-000070	Betterment Traditional IRA 10.1.16 through 12.31.16.pdf
000071-000076	Ally Accounts 12.15.16.pdf
000077-000082	Closing statement marital home 11.8.16.pdf
000083-000087	Ally combined statement 11.15.16.pdf
000088-000091	First Commercial statement 10.17.16 through 11.16.16 showing home downpayment.pdf
000092-000101	First Commercial account 2.17.19 through 3.16.19.pdf
000102-000110	First Commercial account 3.17.19 through 4.16.19.pdf

Sample Bank Subpoena

IN THE __________ COURT OF __________ COUNTY, __________
__________ JUDICIAL DISTRICT

[NAME OF PLAINTIFF] **PLAINTIFF**

VS. **CAUSE NO. ____________**

[NAME OF DEFENDANT] **DEFENDANT**

SUBPOENA DUCES TECUM

WE COMMAND YOU TO SUMMON:

To: **[NAME OF FINANCIAL INSTITUTION]**
C/O [NAME OF REGISTERED AGENT IF APPLICABLE]
[FINANCIAL INSTITUTION ADDRESS LINE 1]
[FINANCIAL INSTITUTION ADDRESS LINE 2]

Pursuant to [Rule of Civil Procedure for Subpoenas], you are to produce the documents listed below by delivering copies of the documents, certified by you to be true and correct copies, to the law offices of [Name and Address of Your Firm], on or before ten days after the date of service.

1. All financial statements for ________ (SS# xxx-xx-[Last Four of Social Security Number]), or any accounts in which ________ has an interest, from [Beginning Date of Requested Info] to present.

2. Checking statements and returned checks for accounts for ________ (SS# xxx-xx-[Last Four of Social Security Number]), or any accounts in which ________ has an interest or is a signatory, from [Beginning Date of Requested Info] through the present.

3. Statements for any and all savings accounts for ________ (SS# xxx-xx-[Last Four of Social Security Number]), or any accounts in which ________ has an interest, from [Beginning Date of Requested Info] through the present.

4. All loan applications or files for loans to ________ (SS# xxx-xx-[Last Four of Social Security Number]), or any accounts in which ________ has an interest, from [Beginning Date of Requested Info] through the present.

5. Documents in your possession regarding any other financial information pertaining to ________ (SS# xxx-xx-[Last Four of Social Security Number]), or any accounts in which ________ has an interest, from [Beginning Date of Requested Info] through the present.

6. Any and all documents evidencing any and all sales of property transactions or loans involving ________ (SS# xxx-xx-[Last Four of Social Security Number]), or any accounts in which ________ has an interest, from [Beginning Date of Requested Info] through the present, including but not limited to all closing documents, loan applications, financial statements, analysis, appraisals, statements, writings, and reports.

You are expected to produce the foregoing documents pursuant to Rule [Rule of Civil Procedure for Subpoenas] of the [State] Rules of Civil Procedure without necessity of an appearance by mailing copies of the documents, certified by you to be true and correct copies, to [Name and Address of Your Firm], on or before the date indicated.

IF WE CAN OBTAIN COPIES OF THESE DOCUMENTS THAT RESPOND TO THIS SUBPOENA, YOUR APPEARANCE WILL NOT BE NECESSARY. PLEASE PROVIDE US WITH AN INVOICE FOR ALL COPY CHARGES.

YOU MUST HAVE THE CUSTODIAN OF RECORDS COMPLETE THE ATTACHED AFFIDAVIT OF RECORDS CUSTODIAN.

HEREIN YOU SHALL NOT FAIL UNDER THE PENALTY IN SUCH CASES PROVIDED; AND HAVE THERE AND THEN THIS WRIT.

You are not required to file an answer or other pleading, but you may do so if you desire.

WITNESS MY SIGNATURE and seal of office, this the _____ day of _________, [year].

[Clerk Name], Clerk
[County Name] County Chancery Clerk

BY: ________________________D.C.

Attorney Name
Firm Name
Address of Firm Line 1
Address of Firm Line 2
Telephone
Telecopier
Email Address
Attorneys for [Client Name]

IN THE __________ COURT OF __________ COUNTY, __________
__________ JUDICIAL DISTRICT

NAME OF PLAINTIFF **PLAINTIFF**

VS. **CAUSE NO. ______________**

NAME OF DEFENDANT **DEFENDANT**

STATE OF ____________________
COUNTY OF ____________________

PERSONALLY appeared before me, the undersigned authority in and for the jurisdiction aforesaid, the within named ________________________, [Affiant's Name], who, after being by me first duly sworn, deposes and says as follows:

1. My name is ________________________.
2. I am the records custodian for **NAME OF FINANCIAL INSTITUTION**. I have firsthand knowledge about the making, maintenance, and storage of documents to which this Affidavit is attached.
3. The documents to which this Affidavit is attached are authentic duplicates of the memoranda, reports, records, and data compilations of acts, events, conditions, opinions, and/or occurrences, made at or near the time of the occurrence of the matters set forth by, or from information transmitted by, a person with knowledge of those matters. These documents are and were made and kept in the course of regularly conducted business activities of **NAME OF FINANCIAL INSTITUTION**. It was and is the regular practice of **NAME OF FINANCIAL INSTITUTION** to make the said memoranda, reports, records, and data compilations.
4. These records are maintained in the form that such records are kept in the regular practice and course of **NAME OF FINANCIAL INSTITUTION'S** regularly conducted activities.

FURTHER, Affiant saith naught.

____
[PLEASE SIGN]

SWORN TO AND SUBSCRIBED BEFORE ME this the _____ day of ___________, [year].

____
NOTARY PUBLIC

My Commission Expires:

<u>CERTIFICATE OF SERVICE</u>

The undersigned counsel does hereby certify that this day a true and correct copy of the foregoing instrument was delivered, via ________, to opposing counsel.

SO CERTIFIED, this the _____ day of ___________, [year].

<u>/s/Attorney Name</u>
Attorney Name

Sample Cellular Carrier Subpoena

IN THE __________ COURT OF __________ COUNTY, __________
__________ JUDICIAL DISTRICT

[NAME OF PLAINTIFF] **PLAINTIFF**

VS. **CAUSE NO. ____________**

[NAME OF DEFENDANT] **DEFENDANT**

SUBPOENA DUCES TECUM

WE COMMAND YOU TO SUMMON:

To: **[NAME OF CELLULAR CARRIER]**
C/O [NAME OF REGISTERED AGENT IF APPLICABLE]
[CELLULAR CARRIER ADDRESS LINE 1]
[CELLULAR CARRIER ADDRESS LINE 2]

Pursuant to [Rule of Civil Procedure for Subpoenas], you are to produce the documents listed below by delivering copies of the documents, certified by you to be true and correct copies, to the law offices of [Name and Address of Your Firm], on or before ten days after the date of service.

1. All records created and/or maintained in the ordinary course of business for the telephone and/or text message service for telephone number ________ and/or accounts for ________ (D.O.B. xx/xx/[year]), including but not limited to detailed billing statements and/or a listing of telephone calls placed and received, a listing of all text messages sent and received, and a printout of all text messages including content sent and received, as well as all fees and charges assessed, from [Beginning Date of Requested Info] through the present.

2. All cell site information, GPS data, cell site data, and any information related to location-based services for telephone number ________ and/or accounts for ________ (D.O.B. xx/xx/[year]), from [Beginning Date of Requested Info] through the present.

You are expected to produce the foregoing documents pursuant to Rule [Rule of Civil Procedure for Subpoenas] of the [State] Rules of Civil Procedure without necessity of an appearance by mailing copies of the documents, certified by you to be true and correct copies, to [Name and Address of Your Firm], on or before the date indicated.

IF WE CAN OBTAIN COPIES OF THESE DOCUMENTS THAT RESPOND TO THIS SUBPOENA, YOUR APPEARANCE WILL NOT BE NECESSARY. PLEASE PROVIDE US WITH AN INVOICE FOR ALL COPY CHARGES.

YOU MUST HAVE THE CUSTODIAN OF RECORDS COMPLETE THE ATTACHED AFFIDAVIT OF RECORDS CUSTODIAN.

HEREIN YOU SHALL NOT FAIL UNDER THE PENALTY IN SUCH CASES PROVIDED; AND HAVE THERE AND THEN THIS WRIT.

You are not required to file an answer or other pleading, but you may do so if you desire.

WITNESS MY SIGNATURE and seal of office, this the _____ day of __________, [year].

[Clerk Name], Clerk
[County Name] County Chancery Clerk

BY: ________________________D.C.

Attorney Name
Firm Name
Address of Firm Line 1
Address of Firm Line 2
Telephone
Telecopier
Email Address
Attorneys for [Client Name]

IN THE __________ COURT OF __________ COUNTY, __________
__________ JUDICIAL DISTRICT

[NAME OF PLAINTIFF] **PLAINTIFF**

VS. **CAUSE NO. ____________**

[NAME OF DEFENDANT] **DEFENDANT**

STATE OF ______________________
COUNTY OF ______________________

PERSONALLY appeared before me, the undersigned authority in and for the jurisdiction aforesaid, the within named ______________________, [Affiant's Name], who, after being by me first duly sworn, deposes and says as follows:

1. My name is ______________________.
2. I am the records custodian for **NAME OF CELLULAR CARRIER**. I have firsthand knowledge about the making, maintenance, and storage of documents to which this Affidavit is attached.
3. The documents to which this Affidavit is attached are authentic duplicates of the memoranda, reports, records, and data compilations of acts, events, conditions, opinions, and/or occurrences, made at or near the time of the occurrence of the matters set forth by, or from information transmitted by, a person with knowledge of those matters. These documents are and were made and kept in the course of regularly conducted business activities of **NAME OF CELLULAR CARRIER**. It was and is the regular practice of **NAME OF CELLULAR CARRIER** to make the said memoranda, reports, records, and data compilations.
4. These records are maintained in the form that such records are kept in the regular practice and course of **NAME OF CELLULAR CARRIER'S** regularly conducted activities.

FURTHER, Affiant saith naught.

____

[PLEASE SIGN]

SWORN TO AND SUBSCRIBED BEFORE ME this the _____ day of ___________, [year].

____

NOTARY PUBLIC

My Commission Expires:

CERTIFICATE OF SERVICE

The undersigned counsel does hereby certify that this day a true and correct copy of the foregoing instrument was delivered, via ________, to opposing counsel.

SO CERTIFIED, this the _____ day of ___________, [year].

/s/Attorney Name
Attorney Name

Sample Counseling Records Subpoena

IN THE __________ COURT OF __________ COUNTY, __________
__________ JUDICIAL DISTRICT

[NAME OF PLAINTIFF]	**PLAINTIFF**
VS.	**CAUSE NO. ____________**
[NAME OF DEFENDANT]	**DEFENDANT**

SUBPOENA DUCES TECUM

WE COMMAND YOU TO SUMMON:

To: **[NAME OF COUNSELOR]**
[NAME OF HOSPITAL/PRACTICE]
[COUNSELOR'S ADDRESS LINE 1]
[COUNSELOR'S ADDRESS LINE 2]

Pursuant to [Rule of Civil Procedure for Subpoenas], you are to produce the documents listed below by delivering copies of the documents, certified by you to be true and correct copies, to the law offices of [Name and Address of Your Firm], on or before ten days after the date of service.

1. Any and all records, notes, materials, evaluations, tests, opinions, narratives, and correspondence pertaining to counseling of _________ (SS# xxx-xx-[Last Four of Social Security Number]), from [Beginning Date of Requested Info] through the present.

You are expected to produce the foregoing documents pursuant to Rule [Rule of Civil Procedure for Subpoenas] of the [State] Rules of Civil Procedure without necessity of an appearance by mailing copies of the documents, certified by you to be true and correct copies, to [Name and Address of Your Firm], on or before the date indicated.

IF WE CAN OBTAIN COPIES OF THESE DOCUMENTS THAT RESPOND TO THIS SUBPOENA, YOUR APPEARANCE WILL NOT BE NECESSARY. PLEASE PROVIDE US WITH AN INVOICE FOR ALL COPY CHARGES.

YOU MUST HAVE THE CUSTODIAN OF RECORDS COMPLETE THE ATTACHED AFFIDAVIT OF RECORDS CUSTODIAN.

HEREIN YOU SHALL NOT FAIL UNDER THE PENALTY IN SUCH CASES PROVIDED; AND HAVE THERE AND THEN THIS WRIT.

You are not required to file an answer or other pleading, but you may do so if you desire.

WITNESS MY SIGNATURE and seal of office, this the _____ day of __________, [year].

[Clerk Name], Clerk
[County Name] County Chancery Clerk

BY: ________________________D.C.

Attorney Name
Firm Name
Address of Firm Line 1
Address of Firm Line 2
Telephone
Telecopier
Email Address
Attorneys for [Client Name]

IN THE __________ COURT OF __________ COUNTY, __________
__________ JUDICIAL DISTRICT

[NAME OF PLAINTIFF] **PLAINTIFF**

VS. **CAUSE NO. ____________**

[NAME OF DEFENDANT] **DEFENDANT**

STATE OF ______________________________
COUNTY OF ______________________________

PERSONALLY appeared before me, the undersigned authority in and for the jurisdiction aforesaid, the within named ________________________, [Affiant's Name], who, after being by me first duly sworn, deposes and says as follows:

1. My name is ________________________.
2. I am the records custodian for **NAME OF COUNSELOR**. I have firsthand knowledge about the making, maintenance, and storage of documents to which this Affidavit is attached.
3. The documents to which this Affidavit is attached are authentic duplicates of the memoranda, reports, records, and data compilations of acts, events, conditions, opinions, and/or occurrences, made at or near the time of the occurrence of the matters set forth by, or from information transmitted by, a person with knowledge of those matters. These documents are and were made and kept in the course of regularly conducted business activities of **NAME OF COUNSELOR**. It was and is the regular practice of **NAME OF COUNSELOR** to make the said memoranda, reports, records, and data compilations.
4. These records are maintained in the form that such records are kept in the regular practice and course of **NAME OF COUNSELOR'S** regularly conducted activities.

FURTHER, Affiant saith naught.

____

[PLEASE SIGN]

SWORN TO AND SUBSCRIBED BEFORE ME this the _____ day of ___________, [year].

____
NOTARY PUBLIC

My Commission Expires:

CERTIFICATE OF SERVICE

The undersigned counsel does hereby certify that this day a true and correct copy of the foregoing instrument was delivered, via ________, to opposing counsel.

SO CERTIFIED, this the _____ day of ___________, [year].

/s/Attorney Name
Attorney Name

Sample Deposition Subpoena

IN THE __________ COURT OF __________ COUNTY, __________
__________ JUDICIAL DISTRICT

[NAME OF PLAINTIFF] **PLAINTIFF**

VS. **CAUSE NO. ____________**

[NAME OF DEFENDANT] **DEFENDANT**

DEPOSITION SUBPOENA

TO: ANY LAWFUL OFFICER OR OTHER PERSON AUTHORIZED TO SERVE SUBPOENAS

WE HEREBY COMMAND YOU TO SUMMON:

[NAME OF PERSON BEING DEPOSED]
[DEPONENT'S ADDRESS LINE 1]
[DEPONENT'S ADDRESS LINE 2]

To be and personally appear for a deposition on __________, at __________ [a.m./p.m.] at the Law Offices [Name of Firm], [Address of Firm] to give evidence in the above styled and numbered cause as set forth in the attached notice.

HEREIN YOU SHALL NOT FAIL UNDER THE PENALTY IN SUCH CASES PROVIDED; AND HAVE THERE AND THEN THIS WRIT.

WITNESS MY SIGNATURE and seal of office, this the _____ day of _________, [year].

[Clerk Name], Clerk
[County Name] County Chancery Clerk

BY: ____________________ D.C.

Attorney Name
Firm Name
Address of Firm Line 1
Address of Firm Line 2
Telephone
Telecopier
Email Address
Attorneys for [Client Name]

CERTIFICATE OF SERVICE

The undersigned counsel does hereby certify that this day a true and correct copy of the foregoing instrument was delivered, via ________, to opposing counsel.

SO CERTIFIED, this the _____ day of ____________, [year].

/s/Attorney Name
Attorney Name

Sample Doctor Records Subpoena

IN THE __________ COURT OF __________ COUNTY, __________
__________ JUDICIAL DISTRICT

[NAME OF PLAINTIFF] **PLAINTIFF**

VS. **CAUSE NO. ______________**

[NAME OF DEFENDANT] **DEFENDANT**

SUBPOENA DUCES TECUM

WE COMMAND YOU TO SUMMON:

To: **[NAME OF HOSPITAL/PRACTICE]**
[HOSPITAL'S ADDRESS LINE 1]
[HOSPITAL'S ADDRESS LINE 2]

Pursuant to [Rule of Civil Procedure for Subpoenas], you are to produce the documents listed below by delivering copies of the documents, certified by you to be true and correct copies, to the law offices of [Name and Address of Your Firm], on or before ten days after the date of service.

1. Any and all records, to or in any way pertaining to ______ (SS# xxx-xx-[Last Four of Social Security Number]), D.O.B. xx/xx/[year], including without restriction all medical histories, intake, records, reports, summaries, diagnoses, prognosis, physician's progress sheets, physician order sheets, nurse's daily notes, records of treatment and medication ordered and given, operative notes, pathology reports, x-ray or radiology reports, and all other written notes, entries, reports, or other written or graphic data prepared, kept, or maintained that pertain to any hospital, emergency room care, physical therapy, or outpatient care for ______, including all outpatient treatments subsequent to the last discharge and any other periods of hospitalization from [Beginning Date of Requested Info] to the present time.

You are expected to produce the foregoing documents pursuant to Rule [Rule of Civil Procedure for Subpoenas] of the [State] Rules of Civil Procedure without necessity of an appearance by mailing copies of the documents, certified by you to be true and correct copies, to [Name and Address of Your Firm], on or before the date indicated.

IF WE CAN OBTAIN COPIES OF THESE DOCUMENTS THAT RESPOND TO THIS SUBPOENA, YOUR APPEARANCE WILL NOT BE NECESSARY. PLEASE PROVIDE US WITH AN INVOICE FOR ALL COPY CHARGES.

YOU MUST HAVE THE CUSTODIAN OF RECORDS COMPLETE THE ATTACHED AFFIDAVIT OF RECORDS CUSTODIAN.

HEREIN YOU SHALL NOT FAIL UNDER THE PENALTY IN SUCH CASES PROVIDED; AND HAVE THERE AND THEN THIS WRIT.

You are not required to file an answer or other pleading, but you may do so if you desire.

WITNESS MY SIGNATURE and seal of office, this the _____ day of __________, [year].

[Clerk Name], Clerk
[County Name] County Chancery Clerk

BY: ________________________ D.C.

Attorney Name
Firm Name
Address of Firm Line 1
Address of Firm Line 2
Telephone
Telecopier
Email Address
Attorneys for [Client Name]

IN THE __________ COURT OF __________ COUNTY, __________ __________ JUDICIAL DISTRICT

[NAME OF PLAINTIFF] **PLAINTIFF**

VS. **CAUSE NO. ____________**

[NAME OF DEFENDANT] **DEFENDANT**

STATE OF ____________________________
COUNTY OF ____________________________

PERSONALLY appeared before me, the undersigned authority in and for the jurisdiction aforesaid, the within named ______________________, [Affiant's Name], who, after being by me first duly sworn, deposes and says as follows:

1. My name is ______________________.
2. I am the records custodian for **NAME OF HOSPITAL/PRACTICE**. I have firsthand knowledge about the making, maintenance, and storage of documents to which this Affidavit is attached.
3. The documents to which this Affidavit is attached are authentic duplicates of the memoranda, reports, records, and data compilations of acts, events, conditions, opinions, and/or occurrences, made at or near the time of the occurrence of the matters set forth by, or from information transmitted by, a person with knowledge of those matters. These documents are and were made and kept in the course of regularly conducted business activities of **NAME OF HOSPITAL/PRACTICE**. It was and is the regular practice of **NAME OF HOSPITAL/PRACTICE** to make the said memoranda, reports, records, and data compilations.
4. These records are maintained in the form that such records are kept in the regular practice and course of **NAME OF HOSPITAL/PRACTICE'S** regularly conducted activities.

FURTHER, Affiant saith naught.

____

[PLEASE SIGN]

SWORN TO AND SUBSCRIBED BEFORE ME this the _____ day of ___________, [year].

____

NOTARY PUBLIC

My Commission Expires:

CERTIFICATE OF SERVICE

The undersigned counsel does hereby certify that this day a true and correct copy of the foregoing instrument was delivered, via ________, to opposing counsel.

SO CERTIFIED, this the _____ day of ___________, [year].

/s/Attorney Name

Attorney Name

Sample Employer Subpoena

IN THE __________ COURT OF __________ COUNTY, __________
__________ JUDICIAL DISTRICT

[NAME OF PLAINTIFF] **PLAINTIFF**

VS. **CAUSE NO. ____________**

[NAME OF DEFENDANT] **DEFENDANT**

SUBPOENA DUCES TECUM

WE COMMAND YOU TO SUMMON:

To: **[NAME OF EMPLOYER]**
C/O [NAME OF REGISTERED AGENT IF APPLICABLE]
[EMPLOYER'S ADDRESS LINE 1]
[EMPLOYER'S ADDRESS LINE 2]

Pursuant to [Rule of Civil Procedure for Subpoenas], you are to produce the documents listed below by delivering copies of the documents, certified by you to be true and correct copies, to the law offices of [Name and Address of Your Firm], on or before ten days after the date of service.

1. All employment records for _______ (SS# xxx-xx-[Last Four of Social Security Number]), including but not limited to job description, travel records, relocation policies, disciplinary records, notes, complaints, payroll, benefits, and/or findings pertaining to his/her employment from [Beginning Date of Requested Info] through the present.

You are expected to produce the foregoing documents pursuant to Rule [Rule of Civil Procedure for Subpoenas] of the [State] Rules of Civil Procedure without necessity of an appearance by mailing copies of the documents, certified by you to be true and correct copies, to [Name and Address of Your Firm], on or before the date indicated.

IF WE CAN OBTAIN COPIES OF THESE DOCUMENTS THAT RESPOND TO THIS SUBPOENA, YOUR APPEARANCE WILL NOT BE NECESSARY. PLEASE PROVIDE US WITH AN INVOICE FOR ALL COPY CHARGES.

YOU MUST HAVE THE CUSTODIAN OF RECORDS COMPLETE THE ATTACHED AFFIDAVIT OF RECORDS CUSTODIAN.

HEREIN YOU SHALL NOT FAIL UNDER THE PENALTY IN SUCH CASES PROVIDED; AND HAVE THERE AND THEN THIS WRIT.

You are not required to file an answer or other pleading, but you may do so if you desire.

WITNESS MY SIGNATURE and seal of office, this the _____ day of __________, [year].

[Clerk Name], Clerk
[County Name] County Chancery Clerk

BY: ________________________D.C.

Attorney Name
Firm Name
Address of Firm Line 1
Address of Firm Line 2
Telephone
Telecopier
Email Address
Attorneys for [Client Name]

IN THE __________ COURT OF __________ COUNTY, __________
__________ JUDICIAL DISTRICT

[NAME OF PLAINTIFF] **PLAINTIFF**

VS. **CAUSE NO. ______________**

[NAME OF DEFENDANT] **DEFENDANT**

STATE OF ______________________________
COUNTY OF ______________________________

PERSONALLY appeared before me, the undersigned authority in and for the jurisdiction aforesaid, the within named ______________, [Affiant's Name], who, after being by me first duly sworn, deposes and says as follows:

1. My name is ________________________.
2. I am the records custodian for **NAME OF EMPLOYER**. I have firsthand knowledge about the making, maintenance, and storage of documents to which this Affidavit is attached.
3. The documents to which this Affidavit is attached are authentic duplicates of the memoranda, reports, records, and data compilations of acts, events, conditions, opinions, and/or occurrences, made at or near the time of the occurrence of the matters set forth by, or from information transmitted by, a person with knowledge of those matters. These documents are and were made and kept in the course of regularly conducted business activities of **NAME OF EMPLOYER**. It was and is the regular practice of **NAME OF EMPLOYER** to make the said memoranda, reports, records, and data compilations.
4. These records are maintained in the form that such records are kept in the regular practice and course of **NAME OF EMPLOYER'S** regularly conducted activities.

FURTHER, Affiant saith naught.

____
[PLEASE SIGN]

SWORN TO AND SUBSCRIBED BEFORE ME this the _____ day of ___________, [year].

____
NOTARY PUBLIC

My Commission Expires:

CERTIFICATE OF SERVICE

The undersigned counsel does hereby certify that this day a true and correct copy of the foregoing instrument was delivered, via ________, to opposing counsel.

SO CERTIFIED, this the _____ day of ___________, [year].

/s/Attorney Name
Attorney Name

Sample Notice of Deposition

IN THE __________ COURT OF __________ COUNTY, __________
__________ JUDICIAL DISTRICT

[NAME OF PLAINTIFF] **PLAINTIFF**

VS. **CAUSE NO. ______________**

[NAME OF DEFENDANT] **DEFENDANT**

NOTICE OF DEPOSITION OF [NAME OF DEPONENT]

PLEASE TAKE NOTICE that the [Plaintiff/Defendant] will take the deposition of [Name of Deponent] as follows:

Date: [Month] [Day], [year]
Time: _____________ [a.m./p.m.]
Place: [Address]

Such deposition may be recorded stenographically and also audio/video recorded and will continue until completion and may be used for trial evidentiary and impeachment purposes. Please take notice the expert witness of the [Plaintiff/Defendant] will be present as allowed by rules.

This the _____ day of ___________, [year].

Respectfully submitted,
[CLIENT'S NAME]

By: /s/Attorney Name
Attorney Name

Attorney Name
Firm Name
Address of Firm Line 1
Address of Firm Line 2
Telephone
Telecopier
Email Address
Attorneys for [Client Name]

CERTIFICATE OF SERVICE

The undersigned counsel does hereby certify that this day a true and correct copy of the foregoing instrument was delivered, via ________, to opposing counsel.

SO CERTIFIED, this the _____ day of ____________, [year].

/s/Attorney Name
Attorney Name

Sample Notice of Inspection

IN THE ___________ COURT OF ___________ COUNTY, ___________
___________ JUDICIAL DISTRICT

[NAME OF PLAINTIFF] **PLAINTIFF**

VS. **CAUSE NO. _______________**

[NAME OF DEFENDANT] **DEFENDANT**

REQUEST TO PERMIT ENTRY UPON LAND FOR THE PURPOSE OF INSPECTION, SURVEYING, PHOTOGRAPHING, AND APPRAISING

COMES NOW the Plaintiff/Defendant, pursuant to [State or Federal] Rule of Civil Procedure 34, and serves this request to permit entry upon land for the purpose of inspection, surveying, photographing, and appraising.

Property description:

The marital home located at ____________________________ and the surrounding property, including ____________________________.

Items to be inspected:

The boundaries for the property and everything located therein including the building and its contents for the purposes of a commercial real estate appraisal.

Date and time of inspection:

[Date] between _____ and ____ [a.m./p.m.]

Persons inspecting:

[Name of Inspection Company], [Address], [Phone Number]

The [Defendant/Plaintiff] and [her/his] attorneys.

This the _____ day of ___________, [year].

Respectfully submitted,
[CLIENT'S NAME]

By: /s/Attorney Name
Attorney Name

Attorney Name
Firm Name
Address of Firm Line 1
Address of Firm Line 2
Telephone
Telecopier
Email Address
Attorneys for [Client Name]

Sample Notice of Supplemental Discovery

IN THE __________ COURT OF __________ COUNTY, __________
__________ JUDICIAL DISTRICT

[NAME OF PLAINTIFF] **PLAINTIFF**

VS. **CAUSE NO. ______________**

[NAME OF DEFENDANT] **DEFENDANT**

NOTICE OF SERVICE OF [DEFENDANT/PLAINTIFF]'S SUPPLEMENTAL RESPONSES TO [PLAINTIFF/DEFENDANT]'S FIRST SET OF INTERROGATORIES AND REQUESTS FOR PRODUCTION OF DOCUMENTS

Notice is hereby given that [Client Name] served [his/her] supplemental responses to [Plaintiff/Defendant]'s First Set of Interrogatories and Requests for Production of Documents on the Counsel for [Name of Opposing Party]: **Bates Numbered Documents XXXXXX–XXXXXX**.

Further notice is hereby given that the original of this discovery pleading is being retained in our file.

This the _____ day of ___________, [year].

Respectfully submitted,
[CLIENT'S NAME]

By: /s/Attorney Name
Attorney Name

Attorney Name
Firm Name
Address of Firm Line 1
Address of Firm Line 2
Telephone
Telecopier
Email Address
Attorneys for [Client Name]

CERTIFICATE OF SERVICE

The undersigned counsel does hereby certify that this day a true and correct copy of the foregoing instrument was delivered, via ________, to opposing counsel.

SO CERTIFIED, this the _____ day of ____________, [year].

/s/Attorney Name
Attorney Name

Sample Pharmacy Records Subpoena

IN THE __________ COURT OF __________ COUNTY, __________
__________ JUDICIAL DISTRICT

[NAME OF PLAINTIFF] **PLAINTIFF**

VS. **CAUSE NO. ______________**

[NAME OF DEFENDANT] **DEFENDANT**

SUBPOENA DUCES TECUM

WE COMMAND YOU TO SUMMON:

To: **[NAME OF PHARMACY]**
C/O [NAME OF REGISTERED AGENT IF APPLICABLE]
[PHARMACY ADDRESS LINE 1]
[PHARMACY ADDRESS LINE 2]

Pursuant to [Rule of Civil Procedure for Subpoenas], you are to produce the documents listed below by delivering copies of the documents, certified by you to be true and correct copies, to the law offices of [Name and Address of Your Firm], on or before ten days after the date of service.

1. Any and all pharmaceutical records pertaining to ________ (SS# xxx-xx-[Last Four of Social Security Number]), D.O.B. xx/xx/[year], including but not limited to the name and amount of prescription medication, the names of prescribing physicians, the cost of prescribed medications, and the dates each prescription was filled from [Beginning Date of Requested Info] to present.

You are expected to produce the foregoing documents pursuant to Rule [Rule of Civil Procedure for Subpoenas] of the [State] Rules of Civil Procedure without necessity of an appearance by mailing copies of the documents, certified by you to be true and correct copies, to [Name and Address of Your Firm], on or before the date indicated.

IF WE CAN OBTAIN COPIES OF THESE DOCUMENTS THAT RESPOND TO THIS SUBPOENA, YOUR APPEARANCE WILL NOT BE NECESSARY. PLEASE PROVIDE US WITH AN INVOICE FOR ALL COPY CHARGES.

YOU MUST HAVE THE CUSTODIAN OF RECORDS COMPLETE THE ATTACHED AFFIDAVIT OF RECORDS CUSTODIAN.

HEREIN YOU SHALL NOT FAIL UNDER THE PENALTY IN SUCH CASES PROVIDED; AND HAVE THERE AND THEN THIS WRIT.

You are not required to file an answer or other pleading, but you may do so if you desire.

WITNESS MY SIGNATURE and seal of office, this the _____ day of __________, [year].

[Clerk Name], Clerk
[County Name] County Chancery Clerk

BY: ________________________D.C.

Attorney Name
Firm Name
Address of Firm Line 1
Address of Firm Line 2
Telephone
Telecopier
Email Address
Attorneys for [Client Name]

IN THE __________ COURT OF __________ COUNTY, __________ __________ JUDICIAL DISTRICT

[NAME OF PLAINTIFF] **PLAINTIFF**

VS. **CAUSE NO. ____________**

[NAME OF DEFENDANT] **DEFENDANT**

STATE OF ____________________________
COUNTY OF ____________________________

PERSONALLY appeared before me, the undersigned authority in and for the jurisdiction aforesaid, the within named ________, [Affiant's Name], who, after being by me first duly sworn, deposes and says as follows:

1. My name is ______________________.
2. I am the records custodian for **NAME OF PHARMACY**. I have firsthand knowledge about the making, maintenance, and storage of documents to which this Affidavit is attached.
3. The documents to which this Affidavit is attached are authentic duplicates of the memoranda, reports, records, and data compilations of acts, events, conditions, opinions, and/or occurrences, made at or near the time of the occurrence of the matters set forth by, or from information transmitted by, a person with knowledge of those matters. These documents are and were made and kept in the course of regularly conducted business activities of **NAME OF PHARMACY**. It was and is the regular practice of **NAME OF PHARMACY** to make the said memoranda, reports, records, and data compilations.
4. These records are maintained in the form that such records are kept in the regular practice and course of **NAME OF PHARMACY'S** regularly conducted activities.

FURTHER, Affiant saith naught.

____
[PLEASE SIGN]

SWORN TO AND SUBSCRIBED BEFORE ME this the _____ day of ____________, [year].

____
NOTARY PUBLIC

My Commission Expires:

CERTIFICATE OF SERVICE

The undersigned counsel does hereby certify that this day a true and correct copy of the foregoing instrument was delivered, via ________, to opposing counsel.

SO CERTIFIED, this the _____ day of ____________, [year].

/s/Attorney Name
Attorney Name

Sample Police Department Records Subpoena

IN THE __________ COURT OF __________ COUNTY, __________
__________ JUDICIAL DISTRICT

[NAME OF PLAINTIFF] **PLAINTIFF**

VS. **CAUSE NO. ____________**

[NAME OF DEFENDANT] **DEFENDANT**

SUBPOENA DUCES TECUM

WE COMMAND YOU TO SUMMON:

To: **[NAME OF POLICE DEPARTMENT]**
[POLICE DEPARTMENT ADDRESS LINE 1]
[POLICE DEPARTMENT ADDRESS LINE 2]

Pursuant to [Rule of Civil Procedure for Subpoenas], you are to produce the documents listed below by delivering copies of the documents, certified by you to be true and correct copies, to the law offices of [Name and Address of Your Firm], on or before ten days after the date of service.

1. Any and all documents and records in the possession, custody, and/or control of the **[NAME OF POLICE DEPARTMENT]** relating to ____________, D.O.B. xx/xx/[year], including but not limited to complaint records, arrest records, intake records, incident reports, photographs, and any other records.

You are expected to produce the foregoing documents pursuant to Rule [Rule of Civil Procedure for Subpoenas] of the [State] Rules of Civil Procedure without necessity of an appearance by mailing copies of the documents, certified by you to be true and correct copies, to [Name and Address of Your Firm], on or before the date indicated.

IF WE CAN OBTAIN COPIES OF THESE DOCUMENTS THAT RESPOND TO THIS SUBPOENA, YOUR APPEARANCE WILL NOT BE NECESSARY. PLEASE PROVIDE US WITH AN INVOICE FOR ALL COPY CHARGES.

YOU MUST HAVE THE CUSTODIAN OF RECORDS COMPLETE THE ATTACHED AFFIDAVIT OF RECORDS CUSTODIAN.

HEREIN YOU SHALL NOT FAIL UNDER THE PENALTY IN SUCH CASES PROVIDED; AND HAVE THERE AND THEN THIS WRIT.

You are not required to file an answer or other pleading, but you may do so if you desire.

WITNESS MY SIGNATURE and seal of office, this the _____ day of __________, [year].

[Clerk Name], Clerk
[County Name] County Chancery Clerk

BY: ________________________D.C.

Attorney Name
Firm Name
Address of Firm Line 1
Address of Firm Line 2
Telephone
Telecopier
Email Address
Attorneys for [Client Name]

IN THE __________ COURT OF __________ COUNTY, __________
__________ JUDICIAL DISTRICT

[NAME OF PLAINTIFF] **PLAINTIFF**

VS. **CAUSE NO. ____________**

[NAME OF DEFENDANT] **DEFENDANT**

STATE OF ____________________________
COUNTY OF ____________________________

PERSONALLY appeared before me, the undersigned authority in and for the jurisdiction aforesaid, the within named ________________________, [Affiant's Name], who, after being by me first duly sworn, deposes and says as follows:

1. My name is ________________________.
2. I am the records custodian for **NAME OF POLICE DEPARTMENT**. I have firsthand knowledge about the making, maintenance, and storage of documents to which this Affidavit is attached.
3. The documents to which this Affidavit is attached are authentic duplicates of the memoranda, reports, records, and data compilations of acts, events, conditions, opinions, and/or occurrences, made at or near the time of the occurrence of the matters set forth by, or from information transmitted by, a person with knowledge of those matters. These documents are and were made and kept in the course of regularly conducted business activities of **NAME OF POLICE DEPARTMENT**. It was and is the regular practice of **NAME OF POLICE DEPARTMENT** to make the said memoranda, reports, records, and data compilations.
4. These records are maintained in the form that such records are kept in the regular practice and course of **NAME OF POLICE DEPARTMENT'S** regularly conducted activities.

FURTHER, Affiant saith naught.

____
[PLEASE SIGN]

SWORN TO AND SUBSCRIBED BEFORE ME this the _____ day of ___________, [year].

____

NOTARY PUBLIC

My Commission Expires:

CERTIFICATE OF SERVICE

The undersigned counsel does hereby certify that this day a true and correct copy of the foregoing instrument was delivered, via ________, to opposing counsel.

SO CERTIFIED, this the _____ day of ___________, [year].

/s/Attorney Name

Attorney Name

Sample Private Investigator Subpoena

IN THE __________ COURT OF __________ COUNTY, __________
__________ JUDICIAL DISTRICT

[NAME OF PLAINTIFF] **PLAINTIFF**

VS. **CAUSE NO. ____________**

[NAME OF DEFENDANT] **DEFENDANT**

SUBPOENA DUCES TECUM

WE COMMAND YOU TO SUMMON:

To: **[NAME OF PRIVATE INVESTIGATOR]**
C/O [NAME OF REGISTERED AGENT IF APPLICABLE]
[PRIVATE INVESTIGATOR ADDRESS LINE 1]
[PRIVATE INVESTIGATOR ADDRESS LINE 2]

Pursuant to [Rule of Civil Procedure for Subpoenas], you are to produce the documents listed below by delivering copies of the documents, certified by you to be true and correct copies, to the law offices of [Name and Address of Your Firm], on or before ten days after the date of service.

1. Any records pertaining to the surveillance of [Name] (D.O.B. xx/xx/[year]), including but not limited to correspondence, telephone conference notes, dates of contact with the hiring party or attorney, payment, notes, videos, and/or findings from [Beginning Date of Requested Info] to present.

You are expected to produce the foregoing documents pursuant to Rule [Rule of Civil Procedure for Subpoenas] of the [State] Rules of Civil Procedure without necessity of an appearance by mailing copies of the documents, certified by you to be true and correct copies, to [Name and Address of Your Firm], on or before the date indicated.

IF WE CAN OBTAIN COPIES OF THESE DOCUMENTS THAT RESPOND TO THIS SUBPOENA, YOUR APPEARANCE WILL NOT BE NECESSARY. PLEASE PROVIDE US WITH AN INVOICE FOR ALL COPY CHARGES.

YOU MUST HAVE THE CUSTODIAN OF RECORDS COMPLETE THE ATTACHED AFFIDAVIT OF RECORDS CUSTODIAN.

HEREIN YOU SHALL NOT FAIL UNDER THE PENALTY IN SUCH CASES PROVIDED; AND HAVE THERE AND THEN THIS WRIT.

You are not required to file an answer or other pleading, but you may do so if you desire.

WITNESS MY SIGNATURE and seal of office, this the _____ day of __________, [year].

[Clerk Name], Clerk
[County Name] County Chancery Clerk

BY: ________________________D.C.

Attorney Name
Firm Name
Address of Firm Line 1
Address of Firm Line 2
Telephone
Telecopier
Email Address
Attorneys for [Client Name]

IN THE ___________ COURT OF ___________ COUNTY, ___________
___________ JUDICIAL DISTRICT

[NAME OF PLAINTIFF] **PLAINTIFF**

VS. **CAUSE NO. ______________**

[NAME OF DEFENDANT] **DEFENDANT**

STATE OF ______________________________
COUNTY OF ______________________________

PERSONALLY appeared before me, the undersigned authority in and for the jurisdiction aforesaid, the within named _________, [Affiant's Name], who, after being by me first duly sworn, deposes and says as follows:

1. My name is ___________________________.
2. I am the records custodian for **NAME OF PRIVATE INVESTIGATOR**. I have firsthand knowledge about the making, maintenance, and storage of documents to which this Affidavit is attached.
3. The documents to which this Affidavit is attached are authentic duplicates of the memoranda, reports, records, and data compilations of acts, events, conditions, opinions, and/or occurrences, made at or near the time of the occurrence of the matters set forth by, or from information transmitted by, a person with knowledge of those matters. These documents are and were made and kept in the course of regularly conducted business activities of **NAME OF PRIVATE INVESTIGATOR**. It was and is the regular practice of **NAME OF PRIVATE INVESTIGATOR** to make the said memoranda, reports, records, and data compilations.
4. These records are maintained in the form that such records are kept in the regular practice and course of **NAME OF PRIVATE INVESTIGATOR'S** regularly conducted activities.

FURTHER, Affiant saith naught.

____
[PLEASE SIGN]

SWORN TO AND SUBSCRIBED BEFORE ME this the _____ day of ___________, [year].

____
NOTARY PUBLIC

My Commission Expires:

CERTIFICATE OF SERVICE

The undersigned counsel does hereby certify that this day a true and correct copy of the foregoing instrument was delivered, via ________, to opposing counsel.

SO CERTIFIED, this the _____ day of ___________, [year].

/s/Attorney Name
Attorney Name

Sample School Subpoena

IN THE __________ COURT OF __________ COUNTY, __________
__________ JUDICIAL DISTRICT

[NAME OF PLAINTIFF] **PLAINTIFF**

VS. **CAUSE NO. ____________**

[NAME OF DEFENDANT] **DEFENDANT**

SUBPOENA DUCES TECUM

WE COMMAND YOU TO SUMMON:

To: **[SCHOOL NAME]**
C/O [NAME OF REGISTERED AGENT IF APPLICABLE]
[SCHOOL ADDRESS LINE 1]
[SCHOOL ADDRESS LINE 2]

Pursuant to [Rule of Civil Procedure for Subpoenas], you are to produce the documents listed below by delivering copies of the documents, certified by you to be true and correct copies, to the law offices of [Name and Address of Your Firm], on or before ten days after the date of service.

1. Any and all school records pertaining to **[Child's initials]**, D.O.B. xx/xx/[year], including but not limited to progress and grade reports, disciplinary actions, attendance records, tardy records, registration forms, and teacher notes from [Beginning Date of Requested Info] through the present.
2. Any and all sign-in/sign-out sheets reflecting when [Parent One's Name] or [Parent Two's Name] has been on the campus of [School Name] during the [2017–2018] school year for any reason.
3. Any and all homework approval sheets for **[Child's initials]**, D.O.B. xx/xx/[year], by [Parent One's Name] or [Parent Two's Name] during the [year] school year.

You are expected to produce the foregoing documents pursuant to Rule [Rule of Civil Procedure for Subpoenas] of the [State] Rules of Civil Procedure without necessity of an appearance by mailing copies of the documents, certified by you to be true and correct copies, to [Name and Address of Your Firm], on or before the date indicated.

IF WE CAN OBTAIN COPIES OF THESE DOCUMENTS THAT RESPOND TO THIS SUBPOENA, YOUR APPEARANCE WILL NOT BE NECESSARY. PLEASE PROVIDE US WITH AN INVOICE FOR ALL COPY CHARGES.

YOU MUST HAVE THE CUSTODIAN OF RECORDS COMPLETE THE ATTACHED AFFIDAVIT OF RECORDS CUSTODIAN.

HEREIN YOU SHALL NOT FAIL UNDER THE PENALTY IN SUCH CASES PROVIDED; AND HAVE THERE AND THEN THIS WRIT.

You are not required to file an answer or other pleading, but you may do so if you desire.

WITNESS MY SIGNATURE and seal of office, this the _____ day of __________, [year].

[Clerk Name], Clerk
[County Name] County Chancery Clerk

BY: _________________________D.C.

Attorney Name
Firm Name
Address of Firm Line 1
Address of Firm Line 2
Telephone
Telecopier
Email Address
Attorneys for [Client Name]

IN THE __________ COURT OF __________ COUNTY, __________
__________ JUDICIAL DISTRICT

[NAME OF PLAINTIFF] **PLAINTIFF**

VS. **CAUSE NO. ______________**

[NAME OF DEFENDANT] **DEFENDANT**

STATE OF ______________________________
COUNTY OF ______________________________

PERSONALLY appeared before me, the undersigned authority in and for the jurisdiction aforesaid, the within named _________, [Affiant's Name], who, after being by me first duly sworn, deposes and says as follows:

1. My name is ________________________.
2. I am the records custodian for **NAME OF SCHOOL**. I have firsthand knowledge about the making, maintenance, and storage of documents to which this Affidavit is attached.
3. The documents to which this Affidavit is attached are authentic duplicates of the memoranda, reports, records, and data compilations of acts, events, conditions, opinions, and/or occurrences, made at or near the time of the occurrence of the matters set forth by, or from information transmitted by, a person with knowledge of those matters. These documents are and were made and kept in the course of regularly conducted business activities of **NAME OF SCHOOL**. It was and is the regular practice of **NAME OF SCHOOL** to make the said memoranda, reports, records, and data compilations.
4. These records are maintained in the form that such records are kept in the regular practice and course of **NAME OF SCHOOL'S** regularly conducted activities.

FURTHER, Affiant saith naught.

____
[PLEASE SIGN]

SWORN TO AND SUBSCRIBED BEFORE ME this the _____ day of ___________, [year].

____

NOTARY PUBLIC

My Commission Expires:

CERTIFICATE OF SERVICE

The undersigned counsel does hereby certify that this day a true and correct copy of the foregoing instrument was delivered, via ________, to opposing counsel.

SO CERTIFIED, this the _____ day of ___________, [year].

/s/Attorney Name

Attorney Name

Part 5

Trial

The Temporary Hearing

The temporary hearing is a hearing held at the outset of the case to put everything in status quo until a full trial can be held. The courts don't want to hold a full hearing, but a lot of issues need to be resolved such as child custody, child support, use of the marital home and cars, temporary alimony, payment of debts, etc. In addition, the temporary hearing is tricky because the attorneys have not had the opportunity to do full discovery before heading into court. As a matter of fact, temporary hearings happen so quickly, attorneys are operating blind on a lot of facts. This means that effort should be made to get as much information as possible within a short time frame. If a temporary hearing goes badly, the case starts out badly, and it is likely the firm will lose a client.

Temporary Hearing Checklist. This is designed to make sure preparation is proper for the temporary hearing. Since the hearings typically take place before discovery, thought should be given to how to make sure the necessary evidence is present on short notice.

Notice to Client of Temporary Hearing. This notice ensures the client is formally noticed of the temporary hearing and given information to help her or him in assisting the attorney in preparation.

Temporary Hearing Checklist

1. Check to make sure summons is to a date certain.
2. Is a court reporter necessary? (In many states, the temporary hearings are not "hearings of record," so a court reporter may not be present. Ask your attorney if there is reason to have a court reporter and, if so, try to get one arranged with the court administrator.)
3. Determine witnesses and issue subpoenas.
    - Should opposing party be subpoenaed because he or she is the only one with wage information?
4. Financial subpoenas to obtain wage and other financial information of the adverse party.
    - To employer of adverse party
    - To banking institutions or other lenders for adverse party
5. Should deposition of adverse party be taken beforehand? (This might be critical if custody is contested.)
6. What is timing of discovery? Can temporary hearing be scheduled after answers to discovery come in?
7. Schedule preparation conference with client.
8. Is financial statement prepared?
9. Send client and witnesses written notice of hearing date.

Notice to Client of Temporary Hearing

DATE
NAME
ADDRESS
CITY, STATE ZIP

Dear _______________:

Your temporary hearing has been scheduled as follows:

Time and Place

Your case will go to trial as follows:

Date:
Time:
Place:
Before:

Temporary Hearings

Nature. The temporary hearing is designed to take care of the parties until the full divorce can be settled or tried. The grounds for divorce are not admissible at the temporary hearing and will not be discussed. The property will not be divided at the temporary hearing. The judge will be concerned only with taking care of immediate financial and other concerns on a temporary basis.

Issues. Issues at the temporary hearing include use of the house and cars, division of personal effects such as clothes, temporary support for parties and children, temporary custody and visitation, temporary maintenance of debt obligations, and so on. Again, the reasons for the divorce are not in issue at the temporary hearing.

Procedure. Although there are times when witness testimony is heard at temporary hearings, the norm is that these hearings are held without testimony. Oftentimes, these hearings take place in the judge's office and the parties are not present. This usually depends on the individual judge and her or his feelings about the issues raised. Most judges like to handle temporary hearings in their office without parties present. Testimony is possible, however, so we must always prepare to put on testimony if necessary. Even if we put on testimony, it is not likely the court will permit the matter to take a long time. The court will likely have several other matters to be heard that day.

Witnesses. Trials are conducted with the testimony of the parties and witnesses. Although there are many exceptions, key testimony cannot be presented by letter or affidavit. Now is the time to let your witnesses and family know about the hearing date.

Documents. We have been assembling documents for your hearing. As with the development of witnesses, this process continues all the time. It is important to have documentary backup of all financial matters. It is helpful to have original documents. Please make sure you have provided us with the latest documents.

Personal Property. Personal property can be temporarily divided at the temporary hearing. Please think about what items you will need and provide us with a list.

Family Support. We believe that family support is important at trial for a lot of reasons. Please talk to your family and friends about attending the hearing—not as witnesses, but for moral support. Anyone who will be testifying cannot be in the courtroom until after he or she is through testifying, so you should ask for support from people who will not be testifying. A word of caution: If family or friends attend for moral support, they will be under an obligation to show proper decorum in court, to be quiet and not react to testimony, and to show civility and courtesy to opposing counsel and party.

The Temporary Hearing Notebook. We prepare for trial using what we call "the trial notebook method." We assemble a hearing notebook that contains information for the hearing, lists of witnesses and documents both sides will use, questions and cross-examination for all witnesses, research on pertinent issues, and so on. We may also prepare research memorandums or a "trial brief" to give the judge pertinent research and arguments.

Your Preparation. We will schedule you in for interviews prior to the hearing. We will prepare your questions and give you a copy so you will see exactly what questions we are going to ask you. We will also prepare you for questions we expect opposing counsel to ask. The financial statement is critical for this hearing. ______________ from our office is responsible for assembling the financial documents. Please provide _________ with up-to-date and accurate budget and financial information.

We know that this is a difficult time for you. Contemplating a hearing is nerve-racking. That is normal. Don't be worried if you are nervous. However, if you feel your worry is starting to get the best of you, give us a call and we will help. We will be calling you in the near future for preparation and scheduling.

Sincerely,

[FIRM NAME]

[ATTORNEY]

Interim Trial Management

At various intervals during a litigated case, it is good to stop and audit the case to make sure that nothing is slipping through the cracks and that preparation is proceeding as it should. This audit is a checklist that can be used for that purpose. The reference in item 4 to the "60-day deadline for expert witnesses" refers to a Mississippi rule requiring the designation of experts 60 days before trial. If there is such a rule with a different deadline in your jurisdiction, substitute that number. If there is no such rule, it is wise to make sure discovery answers regarding experts are supplemented 60 days prior to trial to avoid a discovery violation.

Interim Case Management File Audit

1. Check the complaint and answer and counterclaim and answer, etc.
   - Make sure there are no unanswered claims.
   - List what claims for divorce each party is making.
   - List any odd claims for relief or obviously omitted claims for relief.
2. Examine our discovery to them.
   - Is standard discovery propounded?
   - Are their answers complete? Do we need motion to compel?
   - List witnesses they have listed.
   - List documents they have listed.
3. Examine their discovery to us.
   - Have we given complete answers?
   - List witnesses we have listed.
   - List documents we have listed.
4. If possible, determine the 60-day deadline for expert witnesses, calendar it, and take steps to see that the responsible attorney is aware of it and will comply with it.
   - If not possible, because trial date is not set, calendar a reasonable date for the responsible attorney to address this issue.
5. File maintenance.
   - Note whether the file is in order and the pleadings indexed, and make sure there are no loose documents (everything has a place whether bound down or in a folder).

6. For cases where trial is set.
    - Make sure trial date is calendared with appropriate reminders.
    - Is the case properly set by an order or clerk's docket entry?
    - Double-check expert witness designation deadline.
    - Start trial notebook for attorney.
    - Put lists of witnesses and documents in notebook.
    - Meet with responsible attorney to do preliminary designation of witnesses and documents and make sure it is consistent with discovery answers.
    - Determine if all opposing witnesses have been deposed or interviewed. Make a list of those that have not been and bring to attention of the attorney.
    - Make sure prelim trial prep conference is set with the client.
    - Make sure there is documentation of notice to client and witnesses of trial date.

Calendaring for Trial Preparation

Calendaring for trial preparation ensures a methodical and properly staged final trial preparation. The calendaring of such preparation should be customized in conference with your attorney, but here is a suggested calendaring:

- 90 days out—Begin trial preparation following the 90-day checklist.
- 65 days out—Determine what documents need to be used and whether they need to be authenticated. Issue requests for admissions to the opposing side to admit the authenticity of important documents that cannot be otherwise authenticated.
- 61 days out—Make sure experts have been properly identified and their reports completely provided.
- 60 days out—Determine the legal issues and complete research on each issue.
- 50 days out—Settlement? Courts expect attorneys to attempt to work on settlement or resolve certain issues if possible. This is a reminder to take a look again at settlement and see if something is possible.
- 45 days out—Pretrial conference? Would a pretrial conference be a good idea to narrow issues or find out how the court wants to proceed? For example, how does the court want documents handled: does the court want them premarked? Does the court want a list of documents and objections of each party? Does the court want a separate set of documents?
- 30 days out
    - Audit discovery. Make sure all discovery has been supplemented so all necessary proof can come in without a "timeliness of disclosure" objection. Determine what witnesses and documents the opposing party has identified and make sure proper preparation is in place, such as interviews or deposition.
    - Prepare a list of witnesses and documents and order of proof.
    - Send a notice to the client and witnesses reminding them of the trial and location.
- 15 days out—Finalize exhibit list and witness list.
- 14 days out—Are travel arrangements in place?
- 7 days out—Have all questions been prepared?
- 3 days out—Double-check the status of all pleadings and compliance with prior orders.
- 2 days out—Prepare a proposed judgment.
- 1 day out—Check with the court administrator on the status of the docket. Pack the briefcase.

See checklists that follow, the first from *Forms, Checklists, and Procedures for the Family Lawyer* and the others from Steve Peskind's book *100 Days before Trial*. You should sit with your attorney and go over these checklists and customize them to what is important for your team.

Trial Prep Checklist

Preliminary Client Preparation Interview

Final Client Preparation Interview

Asset Notebook
- Appraisals of Personal Property
- Inventory of Personal Property
- Real Estate Appraisals
- Documents Backing Up Assets
- Asset List
- Financial Statement
    - Prepared
    - Filed
    - Supplemented

Witness Preparation
- Depositions
    - Party
    - Witnesses
- Interviews

Subpoenas
- Adverse Party Employer
- Adverse Party Banks
    - Checking Statements
    - Savings Statements
    - Financial Statements
- Adverse Party Auto Loans
- Adverse Party Expense
    - Charitable Donations
    - Cleaners
- Adverse Party CPAs
    - Tax Records
    - Financial Statements

Trial Subpoenas
- Witnesses
- Documents
  - Latest Checking
  - Latest Financial Statements
  - Latest Stock, IRA Statements
- Mileage and Fees for Adverse Witnesses
- Does Adverse Party Need to Be Subpoenaed?
- Do Documents Need to Be Subpoenaed to Trial from Adverse Party?

Send Witness List to Client

Send Outline of Witness Questions to Client

Exhibits
- Pictures of Client, Children's Baby Books, etc.

Expert Disclosure—60 Days Out
Discovery Supplementation Check—30 Days Out
Attorney's 30-Day Check
Discovery Check
- List Their Witnesses
- List Their Documents
- List Our Witnesses
- List Our Documents
- Request for Admissions Answered

Check Setting of Case for Trial
- Signed Order
- If No Signed Order, Is There Notice To:
  - Opposing Counsel
  - Our Client
  - Witnesses

Create List of Orders and Elements of Each Order

Check with Client to See If All Aspects of Orders Have Been Complied With
May Need to File Motion for Contempt

May Need to Create "What We Want" List
Create Issues List for Judge

Trial Notebook
- Begin Set Up
- Complete Notebook:
  - Identify, Number, and Order Trial Documents
  - Contact Opposing Counsel Regarding Documents to Reach Agreement

Pleadings Check
- List Claims and Counterclaims by Each Party
- Double-Check That Answers Have Been Made

Witnesses
- Letter to Witnesses with Witness Information Sheet
- Arrange Final Witness Interview
- Send Client Information Sheet
- Written Notice of Trial

The Checklists

100-Day Checklist

- ☐ Read the entire case file.
- ☐ Read the statute, case law, and secondary materials.
- ☐ Prepare a case notebook.
- ☐ Diary any critical dates and reminders 14 days, 7 days, and 1 day before the deadline.
- ☐ Prepare an outcome narrative.
- ☐ Prepare a statement summarizing the theory of the case.
- ☐ What is the theme of the case?
- ☐ What grabbers will summarize the theme?
- ☐ Prepare a narrative summarizing the desired outcome of the case.
- ☐ Perform a trial visualization exercise.
- ☐ Use the madman-architect-carpenter-judge exercise.
- ☐ Prepare a mind map of the case.
- ☐ Perform a critical analysis of the opponent's case.
- ☐ Prepare proposed findings of fact and judgment.
- ☐ Prepare a preliminary proof chart.
- ☐ Conduct an organizational team meeting.
- ☐ Block out weekly time between now and the trial.
- ☐ Create a notebook dedicated to preparation prompts.
- ☐ Discuss fees with the client.
- ☐ Confirm fee agreement in writing.
- ☐ Diary fee-compliance review.

90-Day Checklist

- ☐ Diary all deadlines with 14-, 7-, and 1-day reminders.
- ☐ If not already set by court order or court rule, request that the court set deadlines for the following (where appropriate):
  - ☐ completion of initial written discovery
  - ☐ completion of supplemental written discovery
  - ☐ disclosure of all witnesses
  - ☐ disclosure of substance of witness testimony and/or opinions
  - ☐ completion of depositions
  - ☐ production of expert reports/opinions
  - ☐ production of rebuttal or surrebuttal expert reports/opinions
  - ☐ exchange of exhibits
- ☐ Do you have all of the data necessary to support your theory and theme?
- ☐ If not, what is the most efficient way to obtain the information?
- ☐ Conduct a general discovery audit.
- ☐ Have you complied with all written discovery requests?
- ☐ Do you owe any updates to previously answered discovery?
- ☐ Have you timely filed formal objections to improper requests?
- ☐ Have you scheduled any objections for hearing?
- ☐ Have you disclosed all witnesses in writing?
- ☐ Has the opposing party disclosed witnesses?
- ☐ Does the opposing party owe any discovery responses?
- ☐ Do you need any updates to prior discovery responses?
- ☐ Have you requested answers or updates?
- ☐ Have you sent a letter to resolve differences concerning deficiencies?

- ☐ Is a motion to compel production of discovery or disclosures appropriate or necessary?
- ☐ Do you need to depose anyone?
- ☐ Have depositions been scheduled?
- ☐ Is an order to compel depositions necessary?

Discovery Compliance

- ☐ Diary all deadlines with ticklers.
- ☐ Meet with client to allocate responsibility for answers/production.
- ☐ Review client answers.
- ☐ Bates stamp and scan completed production.
- ☐ Serve responses on opposing attorney.

Experts

- ☐ Do you need an expert for
  - ☐ valuation of real estate?
  - ☐ business valuation?
  - ☐ appraisal of personal property?
  - ☐ classification of assets?
  - ☐ tracing contributions of nonmarital property?
  - ☐ proving income?
  - ☐ proving lifestyle?
  - ☐ tax issues?
  - ☐ educating the court on a complex topic?
  - ☐ child development?
  - ☐ child custody?

- [ ] Have you investigated any potential expert?
- [ ] If unknown, have you consulted references?
- [ ] Have you reviewed the potential expert's CV?
- [ ] Have you reviewed the expert's publications?
- [ ] Have you personally interviewed the expert?
- [ ] Have you determined the potential expert's fees?
- [ ] Have you consulted the client about hiring the expert?
- [ ] Do you have an engagement agreement with the expert?
- [ ] Are all disclosure dates known and noted in the diary?
- [ ] Have you prepared a letter to the client confirming the decision to hire (or not) an expert for the case?
- [ ] Have payment arrangements with the expert been made?
- [ ] Has the client paid the expert, or do you have an advance from the client to do so?
- [ ] Has your expert been notified of all deadlines in writing?
- [ ] Has your expert report been produced to the opposing party?
- [ ] Have you received the adverse expert's report?
- [ ] Have you received the adverse expert's CV?
- [ ] Have you investigated the adverse expert's credentials and/or publications?
- [ ] Will you challenge the expertise of the opposing expert?
- [ ] Are there any aspects of the opposing expert report that are subject to a Daubert challenge?
- [ ] Have you set up a meeting with your expert to review the adverse party report?
- [ ] Have you set the deposition of the adverse expert (or decided not to depose the expert)?

- ☐ Do you have to pay the adverse expert for her or his time? If so, have arrangements been made?
- ☐ Have you set up a meeting to prepare your expert for deposition?

Property

- ☐ Has a marital balance sheet been prepared?
- ☐ Have you prepared a discrete notebook or folder for the property?
- ☐ Have all assets been valued?
- ☐ How will you prove asset values?
- ☐ Have you solicited stipulations concerning asset values?
- ☐ Have all valuation experts/reports been disclosed?
- ☐ Are there any claims of dissipation or waste?
- ☐ Have you provided necessary notice to the opposing party?
- ☐ Do you have any asset classification issues?
- ☐ Have you determined your theory regarding asset classification?
- ☐ Is an accounting necessary concerning classification of assets?
- ☐ Have you researched law supporting your theory?
- ☐ Will you want to present a trial memorandum on questions of classification?
- ☐ Do you need an accounting or tracing prepared?
- ☐ Will an expert be necessary/helpful regarding classification issues?

Business Valuation

- ☐ Do you have your business valuation report?
- ☐ Have you produced your report?
- ☐ Are any updates necessary?

- ☐ Do you have the opposing expert report?
- ☐ Have you sent the opposing report to your expert?
- ☐ Are you going to depose the opposing expert?
- ☐ If you are deposing the expert, do you have a date set yet?
- ☐ Do you have time set aside to prepare for the deposition?
- ☐ Will your expert attend the opposing expert deposition? If so, do you have good dates for his or her availability?

Proving Income

- ☐ Do you have current income information?
- ☐ What is your theory regarding income?
- ☐ Are there any undisclosed cash issues?
- ☐ Do you have
    - ☐ current paystubs?
    - ☐ W-2s?
    - ☐ 1099s?
    - ☐ K-1s?
    - ☐ individual tax returns?
    - ☐ business tax returns?
    - ☐ bank statements?
    - ☐ credit card statements?
- ☐ Do you need an expert to support your theory of income?
- ☐ Is any forensic investigation or audit necessary to prove income?
- ☐ Will a lifestyle analysis help prove income?
- ☐ Do you have all necessary records to analyze family expenditures?

- [ ] Do you intend to use a summary?
- [ ] Who will lay the foundation for the summary?
- [ ] Have all data relied on in the summary been tendered to the opposing party?
- [ ] Have you complied with all rules requiring service on summary exhibits on opposing counsel?

Taxes

- [ ] Are any tax issues in controversy?
- [ ] Have you calculated the tax impact of a particular property distribution?
- [ ] Do you need an accountant as a consulting or expert witness?
- [ ] Will the judge take judicial notice of a FinPlan or similar tax-calculation program?
- [ ] Have you solicited stipulations concerning tax calculations or the foundation of a tax report?

Child Custody

- [ ] Review all child custody reports/evaluations.
- [ ] Have you requested the underlying file/testing data of any adverse experts?
- [ ] Do you need an expert to deconstruct any adverse reports?
- [ ] Do you need a consulting expert as a trial consultant?
- [ ] Do you challenge the adverse expert based upon expertise or subject matter?
- [ ] Do you have the adverse expert's CV?
- [ ] Have you obtained any publications of adverse expert's?
- [ ] Should you depose any adverse experts?
- [ ] Assuming you decide to depose the adverse expert, has the date been set?
- [ ] Has time been set aside to prepare for the expert deposition?

- ☐ Who will be your witnesses?
- ☐ Will the children testify or be interviewed by the court?
- ☐ Is a motion necessary to permit the children to testify?
- ☐ Will a guardian ad litem or child representative be necessary?
- ☐ Have you disclosed all of your witnesses?
- ☐ Do you need to update your witness disclosures?
- ☐ Has the opposing party disclosed all witnesses?
- ☐ Has the opposing party's deposition been scheduled?
- ☐ Are any other depositions necessary or advisable?
- ☐ Review all correspondence and journals provided by client.

Evidentiary Planning

Relevance

- ☐ Is the evidence material and probative of an issue in controversy?
- ☐ Is the potential evidence cumulative?

Reliability aka Authentication

- ☐ Have you served a request to admit the genuineness of potential exhibits?
- ☐ Could you use the opposing party's deposition to seek an admission regarding authenticity?
- ☐ Did you receive the potential exhibit in response to a discovery request?
- ☐ If so, can you prove you received the particular document in discovery?
- ☐ Have you solicited a stipulation regarding authenticity and/or admission?
- ☐ Will the court take judicial notice of the authenticity of the exhibit?
- ☐ Is the exhibit self-authenticated under Rule 902(11)?
- ☐ Do you have all certificates to admit business records under Rule 902(11)?

- [ ] Is witness testimony based upon personal knowledge, memory, or sensory observations of the witness?
- [ ] Have you scripted the language to lay foundation through witness testimony?

Substantive Rules

- [ ] What possible objections might the opponent raise to the offer?
- [ ] Is the evidence an out-of-court statement?
- [ ] If it is an out-of-court statement, is it exempt from the hearsay rule as an admission of a party opponent?
- [ ] Is the statement being offered for some reason other than the truth of the matter asserted (notice, knowledge, etc.)?
- [ ] Do any exceptions apply to the out-of-court statement?
    - [ ] excited utterance
    - [ ] present sense impression
    - [ ] state of mind
    - [ ] past recollection recorded
    - [ ] records of regularly conducted activity (business records)
    - [ ] commercial publication
    - [ ] statement against interest
    - [ ] residual exception

60-Day Checklist

- [ ] Review your fee balance.
- [ ] Audit compliance with the fee agreement.
- [ ] Follow up with client if no compliance.
- [ ] Review all pleadings/orders.
- [ ] Do you need to amend or answer any pleadings?
- [ ] Prepare a docket book:
    - [ ] Compile all pleadings and orders.
    - [ ] Prepare docket book index.

- ☐ Do you have all transcripts?
- ☐ Have you abstracted all transcripts?
- ☐ Review and if necessary update the following:
  - ☐ proof chart
  - ☐ theory
  - ☐ theme
- ☐ Interview potential witnesses.
- ☐ Consider the witnesses' demeanors.
- ☐ Do the benefits of witnesses outweigh the risks of using them?
- ☐ Is the witness cooperative?
- ☐ If not cooperative, will the witness actively sabotage the case?
- ☐ Is the witness available to testify?
- ☐ Is the witness subject to a subpoena/compulsory appearance?
- ☐ If the witness is out of state, do the benefits of bringing in the witness warrant the price?
- ☐ Do the benefits of a deposition of an out-of-state witness warrant the costs of traveling to depose the witness?
- ☐ Is a video/closed-feed deposition an option?
- ☐ Can you use a deposition to authenticate potential exhibits?
- ☐ Should you depose any of your own witnesses if potentially unavailable at trial?
- ☐ Do you have any privilege issues to contend with?
- ☐ Do you need to obtain any releases or waivers for the testimony?
- ☐ Do you anticipate any Fifth Amendment issues for your witnesses?
- ☐ Do you expect any Fifth Amendment issues for opposing witnesses?

- ☐ Will you call any child witnesses?
- ☐ Will you have any competency issues?
- ☐ Will you be seeking an in camera interview with the children?
- ☐ Will the opposing party seek an in camera interview?
- ☐ Are any preliminary motions necessary regarding a child witness?
- ☐ Have you disclosed all of your witnesses?
- ☐ Have you received disclosures from the opposing party?
- ☐ Will you depose any adverse witnesses?
- ☐ Have you scheduled those depositions?
- ☐ Are all of your depositions complete?
- ☐ Have you analyzed whether to depose the opposing expert?
- ☐ If you are deposing the opposing expert, have you scheduled the deposition?
- ☐ Schedule time to prepare for the expert deposition.
- ☐ Can you informally interview any witnesses disclosed by the opposing party?
- ☐ Do you need to formally investigate any opposing-party witnesses?
- ☐ Have you discussed the adverse witnesses with your client?
- ☐ Have you sent written confirmation to your witnesses regarding the following?
    - ☐ date and time of the testimony
    - ☐ location
    - ☐ where and when to meet
    - ☐ prearranged date for preparation and rehearsal
    - ☐ general topic of testimony
    - ☐ instructions if contacted by opposing party, attorney, or investigator
    - ☐ explanation regarding subpoena

- ☐ Prepare subpoenas to the following:
  - ☐ ____
  - ☐ ____
  - ☐ ____
- ☐ Are the subpoenas served?
  - ☐ Subpoena served on ____________________________ this date ______________.
  - ☐ Subpoena served on ____________________________ this date ______________.
  - ☐ Subpoena served on ____________________________ this date ______________.

Witness Preparation

- ☐ Compile all documents related to witness testimony, including the following:
  - ☐ information sheet
  - ☐ copies of subpoenas
  - ☐ impeachment materials
  - ☐ witness outline
  - ☐ examination of each witness
- ☐ Prepare outline/structure of direct examination of all witnesses.
- ☐ Reduce outline to headnotes and proofs.
- ☐ Prepare cross-examination questions in rough draft.
- ☐ Rework cross-questions.

Exhibits

- ☐ Compile evidentiary exhibits.
- ☐ Premark exhibits.

- ☐ Copy and bind exhibits.
- ☐ Prepare exhibit list.
- ☐ Prepare blank exhibit list for opposing-party exhibits.
- ☐ Authenticity established?
- ☐ Schedule exhibit conference with opposing counsel.
- ☐ Do you need to ask the court for exhibit conference?
- ☐ Would a demonstrative exhibit clarify witness testimony?
    - ☐ timelines
    - ☐ charts or graphs
    - ☐ blowups
    - ☐ poster boards
    - ☐ PowerPoint
    - ☐ whiteboard or flip chart
- ☐ Are you using any summaries?
- ☐ Have you provided all documents summarized?
- ☐ Who will lay the foundation for the summary?

30-Day Checklist

- ☐ Prepare trial memorandum.
    - ☐ legal research
    - ☐ summary of the issues in dispute
    - ☐ summary of noncontroversial/undisputed facts
    - ☐ summary of witnesses disclosed by both parties
    - ☐ proposed exhibit list
    - ☐ any stipulations already reached or sought

- [ ] Prepare opening statement.
    - [ ] brainstorm grabber
    - [ ] outline
    - [ ] include references to theory and themes
    - [ ] rehearse
- [ ] Prepare closing argument.
    - [ ] written or oral?
    - [ ] include facts, law, and emotion
    - [ ] rehearse
- [ ] Will demonstrative aids help opening or closing?
    - [ ] how to use
    - [ ] when to use
    - [ ] formats (poster board, projection, PowerPoint, etc.)
    - [ ] prepare rough draft of demonstrative
    - [ ] finalize demonstrative aid
- [ ] Consider final pretrial motions.
    - [ ] motion in limine to bar cumulative testimony
    - [ ] motion to bar evidence or issues not properly disclosed
    - [ ] motion to pare down witness list
    - [ ] motion to have the admissibility of prospective evidence ruled on in advance
    - [ ] motion to determine anticipated claims of privilege
    - [ ] motion to take judicial notice of certain evidence
    - [ ] motion for leave to call a witness out of order
    - [ ] motion to bar witnesses from observing other witness testimony
    - [ ] motion to allow an expert witness to observe opposing expert's testimony

- ☐ Prepare for final pretrial. Use the conference to do the following:
  - ☐ solicit stipulations
  - ☐ address evidentiary issues
  - ☐ schedule witnesses
- ☐ Have exhibits been exchanged?
- ☐ Have you reviewed opposing party's proposed exhibits?
- ☐ Discuss with judge preferences with exhibits.
- ☐ Request necessary accommodations for client.
- ☐ Discuss settlement.
- ☐ Have all witnesses been confirmed?
- ☐ Are appointments set for preparation?
- ☐ Use client meeting to discuss the following:
  - ☐ trial procedure
  - ☐ format of testimony
  - ☐ rules regarding objections
  - ☐ possibility of being called as an adverse witness
  - ☐ set up follow-up meeting with client to rehearse the direct examination

Other Witness Preparation

- ☐ Schedule preparation conferences.
- ☐ Discuss wardrobe and demeanor.
- ☐ Discuss trial procedure and protocol.
- ☐ Conduct a field trip to courthouse.
- ☐ Explain lawyer's role at trial.
- ☐ Confirm date, location, and time of testimony.
- ☐ Confirm where and who to meet at courthouse.

- ☐ Explain procedure and objections.
- ☐ Explain the role of the court reporter, bailiff, judge, etc.
- ☐ Order translator (if applicable).
- ☐ Provide rules of effective testimony.
  - ☐ speak loudly and clearly
  - ☐ moderate pace
  - ☐ listen, pause, and then answer
  - ☐ don't guess
  - ☐ what to do if you hear an objection
  - ☐ procedure for forgetfulness
- ☐ Discuss witnesses' direct examination.
  - ☐ overview of topics
  - ☐ procedure for foundations
  - ☐ rectifying mistakes
  - ☐ tell the truth
  - ☐ Fifth Amendment issues?
  - ☐ privilege issues
- ☐ Schedule a dress rehearsal for direct examination/cross-examination.
- ☐ Would a demonstrative aid enhance testimony?
  - ☐ If so, prepare the exhibit.
  - ☐ Explain how to use to client.
  - ☐ Format? (poster board, projector, whiteboard, etc.)

- ☐ Discuss expected cross-examination with the witness.
  - ☐ Answer only the question asked.
  - ☐ Don't argue.
  - ☐ Don't volunteer information.
  - ☐ Don't guess.
  - ☐ Think about the question.
  - ☐ The opposing lawyer is not your friend; don't agree to everything.
  - ☐ Correct mistakes.
  - ☐ Cover likely topics.
  - ☐ Any problems from the deposition to cure?
  - ☐ Remember: you will have an opportunity to redirect witness.
- ☐ Conduct a dress rehearsal.
  - ☐ Find associate or other lawyer to conduct.
  - ☐ Deconstruct with witness.
- ☐ Prepare the expert.
  - ☐ Discuss appropriate demeanor and tone.
  - ☐ Get transcript from the deposition.
  - ☐ Discuss problem areas.
  - ☐ Make sure the CV is updated.
  - ☐ Discuss how you will use demonstrative exhibits.
  - ☐ Review the structure of your direct examination.
  - ☐ Discuss how to handle himself or herself on cross.
  - ☐ Discuss topics likely to be covered on cross.
  - ☐ Discuss the procedure for hypotheticals.

7-Day Checklist

- ☐ Review your calendar.
  - ☐ Any conflicts?
  - ☐ Anything need to be rescheduled?
  - ☐ Have I set aside time after court to deconstruct the day?
  - ☐ Anything I should delegate?

Receivable Review

- ☐ Any settlement offers to review or discuss with your client?
- ☐ Coordinate the team.
- ☐ Who will accompany you to trial?
- ☐ Have you instructed that person?
- ☐ Will someone set up and break down each day?
- ☐ Will you use a technology assistant?
- ☐ Can you get in early to set up?
- ☐ Have you notified your assistant how to update you with daily developments?
- ☐ Who will take your phone calls?
- ☐ Set up an out-of-office email assistant.
- ☐ Who is lined up to handle emergencies?
- ☐ Is someone available to make courthouse deliveries?

Miscellaneous Considerations

- ☐ How will you get to court?
- ☐ What time will you leave to go to court?
- ☐ Where will you have lunch?
- ☐ Will you need cash or change?

- ☐ Is your wardrobe determined?
- ☐ Personal grooming:
  - ☐ hair
  - ☐ nails
  - ☐ laundry or dry cleaning
  - ☐ shoeshine
- ☐ Practice opening and closing.
- ☐ Pack
  - ☐ trial notebook
  - ☐ copies of your exhibits with exhibit list
  - ☐ copies of opponent's exhibits with exhibit list
  - ☐ demonstrative exhibits with copy for court record
  - ☐ cell phone and power cord
  - ☐ laptop with power cord
  - ☐ electrical tape
  - ☐ projector
  - ☐ whiteboard
  - ☐ flip chart
  - ☐ markers
  - ☐ easels
  - ☐ extension cords
  - ☐ legal pads
  - ☐ index cards
  - ☐ sticky notes or flags
  - ☐ extra notepad for the client

- ☐ pens and highlighters
- ☐ paper clips or staplers
- ☐ file folders
- ☐ dictionary
- ☐ evidence reference book
- ☐ statute or code of procedure
- ☐ personal items (glasses, lens cloth, hearing-aid battery)
- ☐ water
- ☐ energy drinks
- ☐ energy snacks

☐ Download file to laptop.

☐ Check in with client.

☐ Prepare trial survival package.

☐ Double-check technology.

☐ Repeat positive affirmations.

☐ Relax!

Concluding the Case Checklist

☐ Review the ruling.

☐ Prepare a checklist with all follow-up tasks to complete:

- ☐ Execute deeds.
- ☐ Prepare title transfers or assignments: stock, vehicles, etc.
- ☐ Do QDROs or transfer of retirement need to be done?
- ☐ Any accounting necessary to implement judgment?

- ☐ Deadlines for posttrial motions or appeal docketed?
- ☐ Necessity of support withholding orders?

☐ Meet with the client to discuss the ruling:

- ☐ advise of implications of ruling
- ☐ next steps/options concerning posttrial motions or appeal
- ☐ tax implications of ruling/divorce
- ☐ changing estate plan
- ☐ cancellation of joint debt
- ☐ significant future dates
- ☐ implications of noncompliance with court order
- ☐ procedure for future modification (and what can be modified)
- ☐ arrangements regarding outstanding fees

☐ Send letter to client confirming options and obligations.

☐ Throw a party for client?

☐ Purge the file.

☐ Return originals to client.

☐ Shred duplicates.

☐ Send thank-you notes/acknowledgments.

☐ Keep a journal.

Child Support Calculation

It is helpful to attorneys for you to prepare a proper child support calculation. These calculations obviously vary from state to state, but here is an example of how this can be done to help your attorney. First, get a year-to-date pay stub from the client. In addition, get the previous year's tax return and W-2 or 1099s. Use the year-to-date pay stub if it appears to be accurate given the entire prior year. If the payor is paid on a schedule that is not monthly, you must remember to convert those amounts as follows:

- Paid weekly, multiply by 4.33
- Paid biweekly, multiply by 2.16
- Paid on the 1st and 15th or on the 15th and 30th/31st, multiply by 2

The following is an example of a child support calculation based on biweekly pay:

Income	
Gross Pay Biweekly	$4,788
Biweekly Calculation	2.16
Gross Monthly Pay	$10,342.08
Deductions	
Retirement	$59.28
FERS/TSP	$750.00
Social Security	$283.69
Federal Tax	$640.92
State Tax SC	$248.54
Medicare	$66.35
Total Deductions Biweekly	$2,048.78
Biweekly Calculation	2.16
Total Monthly Deductions	$4,425.36
Adjusted Monthly Gross Income	$5,916.72
Child Support Calculation	14%
Total Monthly Child Support	$828.34

The Fact Sheet

I find it helpful to have a "fact sheet." The fact sheet contains basic but specific information to support the lawyer prior to conferences with the client, depositions, hearings, or trials. The fact sheet should be stapled on the inside leaf of a paper file or placed in a prominent position in the lawyer's notes or notebook. The fact sheet should be customized to each lawyer but should usually contain at least the following information:

- Style of case
- Judge
- Names and ages of the parties
- Date of marriage
- Names and birthdates of children
- Occupations and incomes of each party
- Date of separation
- Important procedural dates, such as:
    - Date of filing of complaint
    - Date of answer/counterclaim
    - Date of temporary order

Trial Preparation Overview

Preparing for trial is like producing a movie. It involves bringing a lot of parts and people together at the right time. It begins at the outset of the case with proper interview techniques and development of strategy and continues all the way through with proper use of discovery and staging of preparations. The trial preparation checklist contains all of the elements of proper trial preparation from start to finish.

Trial Preparation Checklist

- *Preliminary Client Preparation Interview.* Client preparation entails defining the client's position and plotting a course to get the desired outcome. It involves a preliminary preparation of the testimony and decision-making as to witnesses and documents. This should take place anywhere from 90 to 30 days out from trial.
- *Final Client Preparation Interview*
    - Final client preparation should take place close to trial but not the day before. Timing depends upon the attorney. One week ahead of time is a good amount of time, and time should be left open on the day before trial for final review.
- *Asset Notebook.* The "asset notebook" is designed to bring a list of the assets together with documentation of each asset and liability and value. This can contain:
    - Appraisals of Personal Property
    - Inventory of Personal Property
    - Real Estate Appraisals
    - Documents Backing Up Assets
    - Asset List
    - Financial Statement
- *Witness Preparation.* A case might start out with quite a few persons listed as potential witnesses. In the last 60 to 90 days, this list should be narrowed down to the "will call" witnesses, with also a list of "may call" witnesses.
    - *Depositions.* A deposition of the opposing party is a must and should take place in every case. Timing of this deposition can be tricky. If the deposition is taken too late, there may not be time to adjust to the claims. On the other hand, if it is taken too early, the case may have changed drastically after the deposition. One should err on the side of early so the positions of the opposing party can be determined and dealt with in other discovery.
    - *Witnesses.* Depositions of your own witnesses are rarely taken unless there is a need to preserve testimony. Depositions of the other party's witnesses will likely be scheduled relatively late in the process so it is known which opposing witnesses are "will call" witnesses. The attorney should work with the client to find out which of the other side's witnesses need to be deposed.

- *Interviews.* Favorable witnesses should be interviewed once a trial is set and then refreshed in the weeks or days approaching trial. This can be done by phone or in person. A good way for the paralegal to help the lawyer is to set aside a block of time about 30 days out from trial for the attorney to interview all favorable witnesses at once, one after the other. A good practice is for the attorney to prepare the questions and answers from these interviews and then send them to the witness for comment and preparation.
- *Subpoenas.* Subpoenas are a critical part of trial preparation. Properly directed subpoenas obtain authenticated and accurate documentation. Once documents are subpoenaed and an affidavit of authenticity is signed, the documents can be introduced as "self-authenticating."
    - *Adverse Party Employer.* A subpoena for information from the opposing parties' employer is almost essential in every case. This subpoena procures accurate wage information, documentation of work duties and hours, and possible information about disciplinary issues.
    - *Adverse Party Banks.* Subpoenaing bank documents for the adverse party is essential. These subpoenas procure obvious documents such as checking and savings to show spending and assets, but also possible financial statements that may assist in verification of the opposition's assets.
    - *Adverse Party Auto Loans.* A subpoena for an auto loan file can reveal representations by the opposing party as to income and assets.
    - *Adverse Party CPAs.* If necessary, the adverse parties' CPA can be subpoenaed to produce tax records, supporting documents, and financial statements.
- *Trial Subpoenas.* Determination should be made about 45 days out on what subpoenas should be issued for trial preparation or proof purposes.
    - Witnesses
    - Subpoenas duces tecum to update previously obtained information
        - Latest Checking
        - Latest Financial Statements
        - Latest Stock, IRA Statements
    - *Mileage and Fees for Adverse Witnesses.* Be careful when issuing subpoenas to adverse witnesses that the subpoena is accompanied by proper witness and mileage fees if required by statute or rule.
    - *Does Adverse Party Need to Be Subpoenaed?* This might sound strange, but it may be necessary to subpoena the adverse party, either to make sure she or he is there to testify or to bring documents along.
- *Send Witness List to Client.* It is a good idea to send a list of witnesses to the client for approval. That way he or she can assist in making sure the best witnesses are listed and also will know he or she has had a hand in the final preparation.
- *Exhibits.* The attorney should develop a document list early on in the course of the case and revisit the list as the case is developed. Work with the client to refine the list.

- *Expert Disclosure.* Discovery and other rules require the detailed disclosure of expert witnesses and their opinions. The attorney should identify the need for experts early on in the case, and care should be taken to make sure disclosure to the other side is timely and complete.
- *Discovery Supplementation Check—30 Days Out.* Discovery comes with an obligation to update answers as they might change. This is called "supplementation." Care should be taken to supplement discovery as the case proceeds to make sure there is disclosure of all information so that there is no basis for an objection on the ground of nondisclosure or late disclosure.
- *Discovery Check.* The paralegal can assist the attorney by monitoring the discovery and its supplementation by both sides. Keep a particular eye on the following:
    - List Their Witnesses
    - List Their Documents
    - List Our Witnesses
    - List Our Documents
    - Request for Admissions Answered
- *Check Setting of Case for Trial.* It is good policy to always be certain the case is properly set for trial. Make sure there is an order setting the case for trial or a proper entry on the record by the court administrator.
- *Create List of Orders and Elements of Each Order.* A good policy is to make a list of orders and the elements of the order. The purpose is to monitor compliance by either side with the order.
- *May Need to Create "What We Want" List.* At least a week before trial, the attorney should develop with the client a list stating exactly what the client wants. This should be sent to the client for approval so there is no question that the attorney is seeking what the client wants.
- *Create Issues List for Judge.* A good policy is to create a list of issues for the judge. If a pretrial order is not part of the court's normal procedure, this can give the judge a good preview of what she or he is about to hear.
- *Trial Notebook.* Each attorney has different methods for putting together trial preparation. A "trial notebook" is an excellent method. The trial notebook is a three-ring notebook with dividers for facts, witness and document lists, summary of procedural posture, witness questions, and research. The trial notebook can serve as a platform for bringing all of the pieces of trial preparation together. In today's age, attorneys may use their iPads or laptops for this.
- *Pleadings Check.* In the 30 days before trial, the paralegal should do a double check of the pleadings to make sure they are in order. List claims and counterclaims by each party. Double check that answers have been made.
- *Witnesses.* The paralegal should make sure all friendly witnesses are fully informed of the trial date and when they might be expected to testify.

Trial Notebook Requirements

The notebook should be a two- or three-ring notebook of appropriate size for the case. It is to be started at least 30 days before trial. It must be completed by 12:00 noon on the day before trial.

Tabs should be prepared for each section. The tabs should be typed on each side of the tab so that the writing may be read from the ring side of the paper. The notebook should have the following sections:

- Facts
- Pretrial
- Witness list
- Document list
- Witnesses in order of appearance or alphabetical
- Other witnesses
- Research
- Closing
- Paper (the notebook should have an ample amount of lined paper for use during trial)

The Sections

Facts. A typed set of facts must be prepared, including names of parties and children, length and date of marriage, ages of children, incomes of each party, and an asset list.

Pretrial. A list of matters to take up before trial should be made. This should include witnesses to be called, documents to be agreed upon, documents to be premarked, evidentiary problems of rulings, calling witnesses out of order, keeping experts in the courtroom, and so on.

Witness list. A list of each party's witnesses should be made. Our list of witnesses should include their phone number and an indication of whether they have been subpoenaed or will appear voluntarily. Our witnesses should be listed in order of appearance at trial. Their witnesses should be listed in suspected order of appearance.

Documents. A list of documents for each party should be prepared. Our documents should be listed in order of use. This will be determined from each witness's prepared testimony. A trial documents file should be established based upon this list. The trial documents folder should have the original and three copies of the document.

Witnesses in order of appearance. In each witness section the following should be included: typed list of questions, deposition transcript, notes of interviews, copies of documents for use in trial (if feasible), and an extra two pages of notebook paper.

Note: Parties should have their 8.05s in their sections. Note: It is firm policy never to ask a question to which the answer has not been preestablished. In cross-examination, it is firm policy that the deposition of a witness must be carefully studied in preparation for trial. Questions for cross must come from the deposition. When preparing the cross, each question must begin with something like, "Is it true that . . . ." Following the question, the page and line of the answer should be typed. In a copy of the deposition transcript, the pertinent testimony should be highlighted.

Other witnesses. This section is for witnesses that may be called as rebuttal witnesses or surprise witnesses. A couple of sheets of paper should be placed in this section.

Research. Pertinent research on key points of trial should be assembled in this section. The case from West Reporting should be included. A yellow sticky should be placed on the case with a one-sentence statement of its holding and a reference to the page where the pertinent text is. The pertinent text should be highlighted.

Closing. A couple of sheets of paper should be placed here for closing notes.

Making Sure Client and Witnesses Are Prepared for Trial

A key role for the paralegal in preparation for trial is making sure the client and witnesses are advised of the time and place of trial and how to conduct themselves.

Letter or Email Notifying Client of Trial

Dear ________________:

The enclosed Order Setting Time and Place for Hearing was received by us on ______________.

Time and Place

Your case will go to trial as follows:

Date:

Time:

Place:

Before:

Preparation

Witnesses. Trials are conducted with the testimony of the parties and witnesses. Although there are many exceptions, key testimony cannot be presented by letter or affidavit. By now, we have identified key witnesses for your trial. However, we never stop developing essential testimony. If you are aware of any key witness, please make sure you have disclosed that witness to us. If there is a witness you have previously identified, and whom you want us to interview or depose, please let us know that now. Now is also the time to let your witnesses and family know about the trial date and that we will want to interview them in the future; they can assist in this process by calling us to let us know when it will be convenient to talk. We will also send them a letter with some instructions and a request that they call us.

Documents. We have been assembling documents for your trial. As with the development of witnesses, this process continues until the end of the trial. It is important to have documentary backup of all financial matters. It is helpful to have original documents. If the financial documents you have already provided have been updated or superseded, please provide us with the latest documents.

Appraisals. All property must be appraised or properly valued by the parties. If you are aware of any property not so valued or appraised, we need to discuss this immediately and determine if we need to request an appraisal. Appraisals may be avoided if the parties agree on a value.

Personal Property. All personal property, such as furniture, paintings, lamps, washers and dryers, televisions, and stereos, must be inventoried and appraised for trial. The best method for this is to hire a personal property appraiser. At the least, you must prepare a list and place values on each item.

Family Support. We believe that family support is important at trial for a lot of reasons. Please talk to your family and friends about attending the trial—not as witnesses, but for moral support. Anyone who will be testifying cannot be in the courtroom until after he or she is through testifying, so you should ask for support from people who will not be testifying. A word of caution: If family or friends attend for moral support, they will be under an obligation to show proper decorum in court, to be quiet and not react to testimony, and to show civility and courtesy to opposing counsel and party.

The Trial Notebook. We prepare for trial using what we call "the trial notebook method." We assemble a trial notebook that contains information for trial, lists of witnesses and documents both sides will use, questions and cross-examination for all witnesses, research on pertinent issues, and other important information. Our policy is to interview or depose every material witness for trial and to prepare every single question we will ask of any witness. Every document for use at trial will be identified and numbered. We will attempt to work with opposing counsel to identify all documents for use at trial and to prenumber them. This saves time and trouble at trial. We may also prepare research memorandums or a "trial brief" to give the judge pertinent research and arguments in advance of trial. This is tedious and expensive.

Key Dates. The setting of a case for trial creates several key dates in the system. Some of those dates are as follows:

- 60 days from trial. Expert witnesses must be identified to the court and opposing counsel. We will conduct a "60-day meeting" in our office to outline strategy, review deadlines, and conduct preliminary identification of trial witnesses and issues.
- 30 days from trial. We will conduct a "30-day meeting" of all pertinent staff to construct the trial notebook and plan its final preparation. Subpoenas for information or witnesses or documents are discussed at this meeting. Trial preparation times are blocked out for lawyers, and appointments are scheduled for witness interviews. Discovery answers by each party are audited, and we will determine what discovery answers we have made that require supplementation. (If a party does not disclose witnesses, documents, or evidence she or he intends to use at a trial in a reasonable fashion in response to proper inquiry, the evidence may not be allowed.)
- 10 days from trial. This is a key date for final decisions on issuing subpoenas for witnesses or documents because the rules require 10 days' notice on a request for a document pursuant to a subpoena.
- Final days. We will schedule you in for interviews prior to trial. We prefer two interviews in preparation for trial: one several days before trial and then a final preparatory interview a day or two before trial. We will prepare your questions and give you a copy so you will see exactly what questions we are going to ask you. We will also prepare you for questions we expect opposing counsel to ask.

We know that this is a difficult time for you. Contemplating trial is nerve-racking. That is normal. Don't be worried if you are nervous. However, if you feel your worry is starting to get the best of you, give us a call and we will help. We will be calling you in the near future for preparation and scheduling.

Sincerely,

[FIRM NAME]

[ATTORNEY]

Trial Tips for Clients

Preparation

Preparation is the key to successfully presenting accurate information in court. Our office will schedule one or two trial preparation conferences. One conference will be a week or so beforehand to make preliminary preparations. We also like to meet with our clients for an hour or two on the day prior to trial. In the final conference, we will conduct a dress rehearsal of your testimony. At the conclusion of the interview, you will be given an outline of the questions you will be asked.

Depositions: If the opposing party has taken your deposition, it is important to read your deposition carefully. When the opposing counsel is cross-examining you, we may ask you the same or similar questions as those asked in your deposition. If you answer the question differently, opposing counsel will use the deposition to show the court that you have changed your answer. This is called "impeaching" a witness. If you see that your answer at trial might be different than in your deposition, please advise your lawyer of that in one of your trial preparation conferences.

Suggestions: You can be a big help in preparation. You should make lists of suggested questions for yourself and for the opposing party and for witnesses.

Dress Rehearsal: If you would like, one of our staff members will be happy to accompany you to the courtroom in advance of trial so you can become familiar with the setting. This type of dress rehearsal can reduce anxiety and create a feeling of confidence.

What to Wear?

Court is a somber, conservative, and noncolorful environment, so the dress should be consistent with that. Solid navy-blue outfits are almost always appropriate.

Neither men nor women should wear expensive or excessive jewelry. Men should wear one simple ring and a simple watch. Women should wear a ring, a simple watch, and perhaps a simple bracelet or necklace. Earrings may be worn, but they should not be expensive or dangling. Hairstyles for men and women should be conventional.

When to Arrive?

Arrive one-half hour early. Court usually starts at 9:00 in the morning for regular trials. We prefer our clients arrive at least one-half hour early. **YOU MUST NOT BE LATE FOR COURT AT ANY TIME.**

Security

Courts have a similar security requirement to airline travel. Do not bring weapons, guns, knives, or mace to court. Some courts do not permit cell phones or purses.

What Happens When You Get There?

It is typical that the time shortly before the trial is somewhat hectic and disorganized. This is normal. Do not be alarmed by it. There may be several cases or "motions" that are also set for that day, so other lawyers, parties, and witnesses may be there at the same time, milling about. Your attorney may be involved in conversations with court personnel or with lining up witnesses. There may also be some time for a little more preparation.

Typically, the judge asks to see the lawyers for each party in the judge's office. The purpose is to find out about the case, what issues are to be decided, and how the trial is to be managed. The court may also explore a settlement. As a matter of fact, it is quite common that extensive settlement negotiations are conducted on the day of trial with the assistance of the court. Many times, cases are settled on the day of trial, and no testimony is ever presented.

Settlement on the day of trial is so common that it bears further discussion. When the judge hears from the lawyers about what facts may be presented at trial, he or she gives the lawyers guidance as to how he or she might rule. The lawyers use this guidance to formulate appropriate settlement positions for their clients. You should understand, however, that the court is rarely actually deciding an issue or "prejudging" the case. And, settlement on the day of trial is just that, settlement. You always have the option of deciding not to settle any issue on the day of trial. If you feel any pressure to settle, please advise your lawyer.

Conduct at Trial

You should conduct yourself in court the same way you would at any formal occasion. You should not be boisterous or engage in joke-telling or laughing. You should not curse, either on the stand or in and around the courthouse. You should be in complete control of your demeanor and your emotions. Do not react to the other party or to any testimony you hear or to rulings made by the court. The court will be watching how you conduct yourself. Avoid making facial expressions, shaking your head, glaring, scoffing, wincing, wiggling, or making sounds.

If you need to communicate with your lawyer, write a note on a piece of paper and pass it to her or him. Communication is important, but take care to make the communication discreet and not so frequent that it becomes distracting to the lawyer.

Completely avoid using gum, hard candy, chewing tobacco, or snuff in the courthouse.

Witnesses

Witnesses who are friendly to your case do not necessarily need to be subpoenaed, unless they need one to be excused from work or school. Although witnesses should be present at the beginning of trial, it is usually possible to allow them to wait until their turn, provided they are available to respond by phone and travel to the courthouse on short notice.

Children

The courts often have special rules for children testifying. Children may testify in open court. The younger the child, however, the more likely that special accommodation is made. The matter is handled in a number of different ways. It is most common for the court to interview child witnesses in the judge's office in the presence of the attorneys, but not the parties. Courts are aware that children may be very uncomfortable testifying in front of their parents.

Order of Proof

The plaintiff gets to put his or her proof and witnesses on first. Then the defendant goes. The plaintiff may conclude with what is known as "rebuttal." The plaintiff gets the last word. If you are a defendant, do not worry too much about this advantage. The court is aware that you do not have this opportunity. You may be called to the stand as a part of the other party's case. This is known as being called as an "adverse witness." For example, a plaintiff might call the defendant as the very first witness in the case. If this happens to you, do not be alarmed by it. The key is that you are now aware beforehand that it could happen.

Order of Questioning

When a party puts a witness on the stand, that witness is subjected to what is known as "direct examination." During this portion of the examination, the attorney must ask questions in a way that does not suggest the answer. When the direct examination is complete, the other attorney has the right to ask questions during the phase known as "cross-examination." Cross-examination can be somewhat difficult. The cross-examiner has a wide latitude in the subject and manner of questioning. An effective cross-examiner will use "leading questions," that is, questions that suggest the answer, such as "Isn't it true that . . . ." When cross is finished, the other lawyer has the right to ask more questions in what is known as "redirect." On occasion, the judge will ask questions. Do not be alarmed if this happens.

Taking the Stand

When you take the stand, you will be given an oath by the courtroom deputy or bailiff. Afterward, take your seat and look kindly at the judge. Sit comfortably, leaning forward slightly with your feet on the floor. Do not cross your legs, lean back, move back and forth, or slouch. Your job is to listen carefully to the question and respond accurately.

Testifying

When being asked a question, look at the person asking the question. When answering, look at the judge. The judge is the one you are communicating to, not the attorney asking the questions. When opposing counsel is questioning you, look at him or her, but do not become transfixed. Again, remember that your purpose is to communicate with the judge, not to impress or beat or outsmart the opposing counsel. Take your time. There is no hurry. This is not a test, and you are not being graded for the speed of your answers. If you do not understand a question, say so. Make sure you understand exactly what is being asked. If you do not recall something, state that you do not recall. Opposing counsel may try to get you to speculate or guess. Do not fall into that trap, but you must also avoid being difficult as a witness. When answering questions, try to answer the question, first by saying yes or no, if that is what is called for. After answering, begin explaining or qualifying your answer. A witness who refuses to answer questions directly appears to be avoiding the truth.

If you are asked if you have talked to anyone about your testimony or your case, answer, "Of course, I have talked with my attorney." Then say whom else you have talked to. Many people fear this question and the answer. Don't. There is nothing wrong with talking to people about your case, and it is appropriate, of course, to prepare for trial with your attorney.

When answering, do not say "uh huh" or simply nod your head. You must say yes or no. The reason is that the court reporter must record your testimony.

Do not talk too fast. This makes it difficult for the reporter to transcribe your testimony. Don't talk too slowly, as that may appear unnatural.

Do not talk when someone else is speaking. Wait for the questioner to finish the question.

Do not argue. Do ask questions. If you have a question, say, "I don't understand," and say why.

Under no circumstances should you lose your temper. If you have emotion about something, it is appropriate to display it, but never attempt to show emotion because you think it will help. Try to avoid too much crying. Judges can be turned off by too much emotion or crying, and some judges have been known to direct witnesses to stop crying.

When there is an objection, stop talking. The judge will rule on the objection and instruct you whether or not and how to answer the question.

A common objection is to "hearsay." Hearsay consists of out-of-court statements that are made for the truth of the matter asserted. Simply, it consists of what someone told you. Do not worry too much about whether what you have to say is hearsay. That is a complicated legal determination. But once a court sustains an objection to hearsay, you must avoid telling what someone told you. Failure to respect the court's ruling can give the court the impression you do not respect it.

Do not argue with the judge or address questions to her or him.

If you are asked a question that may require you to answer about a possible crime, say, "I'm not sure how to answer that, may I confer with my attorney?" The most common questions in family law cases that deal with crimes are the use of drugs or questions dealing with failure to report income on income tax returns.

Be prepared to tell the court exactly what you want. Do not say "noble" things like "I just want what's fair." You must say what you want.

Sequestration

There is a rule in court called the "rule of sequestration," or simply the "rule." What that means is that witnesses other than the parties are prohibited from hearing the testimony of other witnesses before they testify. The rule is invoked in most cases. This means that the witnesses who have not testified will be kept out of the courtroom. During lunch or overnight, or during other breaks, you and your witnesses must avoid talking about the case. If you do that, the entire trial could be jeopardized. Once a witness has testified, he or she can remain in the courtroom and discuss the case with you.

Support

A trial is a very difficult thing. We recommend that our clients bring a group of supporters to the trial. This group can consist of parents, sisters and brothers, neighbors, people from work, or other friends. This group of people serves many purposes. First, it serves as moral support. Second, it shows the other side and the court that you have good people on your side. It can also be somewhat intimidating to the other side. When bringing your support group, make sure they are aware of the rules stated here. They, too, should avoid showing emotion or hostility, or making faces or gestures in the courtroom.

Conduct in the Courthouse

Remember, when you are in the courthouse or around it, court personnel or people connected with the other side may be watching or hearing you. Conduct yourself as though you are on camera. You must assume that anything you say or do will be observed and heard.

Court Personnel

The personnel of the court, such as the bailiff and court reporter, are often friendly and interested in you. You may talk to them, but do not put on an act for them. They do not make the decisions and have no input into the decisions.

Conduct of the Attorneys

Attorneys and litigants are expected to conduct themselves with courtesy and civility. Many attorneys know each other well. And whether attorneys know each other or even like each other, you may see the attorneys acting very friendly with each other. This is not something to be concerned about. As a matter of fact, the better the lawyers, the more likely it is that they will treat each other with a great deal of courtesy.

The Ruling

In relatively small cases, it is not unusual for the judge to render a ruling at the end of the trial. However, in cases that are difficult or complicated, it is common for the court to "take the matter under advisement." It is common in those cases for the court to ask the lawyers to prepare suggested findings for the court to read.

After Trial

If there is some animosity between the parties, this should not be exhibited in the courtroom. It is OK in these circumstances to exit the courtroom and the courthouse at different times, in order to avoid difficult or awkward circumstances.

Are We Winning?

A trial can be like a prize fight. Punches are thrown by each side. Both parties get bruised. The real "winner" is not known until the end. Often, you cannot tell how you are doing. When you put on your side of the case, you often feel like you are "winning." When the other side puts on their case, one often feels that the other side is "winning." Do not fall into this trap. Don't try to anticipate the result. I often tell clients that I judge myself only by whether I planned the case properly and achieved what I set out to achieve in the case. If I do that, I cannot worry about the result and must have faith.

Letter or Email to Trial Witnesses

Dear ______________:

We appreciate your taking the time to discuss the above-referenced case with us. As you know, you have been named as a trial witness by ______________in the divorce case currently set for trial on __________________, in __________________, before the Honorable ________________. The address is: ______________________________

We would appreciate your being on standby to testify on any one of these days, if possible. However, we will do everything in our power to schedule your testimony for ____________________.

If you have any questions or think of any additional information of which we should be aware, please give [ATTORNEY] or me a call. We thank you again for your courtesy and cooperation.

Sincerely,

[FIRM NAME]

[ATTORNEY]

Enc. To Our Friends

Trial Instruction Sheet to Friends of Client

To Our Friends

We appreciate your agreeing to attend trial to support our client. Trials are very difficult. They exact a huge emotional toll on the participants. Litigants often feel that their very life is at stake. Your support is greatly appreciated and helpful.

This memo is designed to answer general questions you may have. Shortly before trial, our office will schedule a brief telephone conference with you to discuss any specific concerns you may have.

Make plans to meet us at the courthouse (or other designated location) a half-hour before trial. Court usually starts at 9:00 A.M. for regular trials. We realize that you may be taking time from your job or other obligation to support your friend. We will make every effort to eliminate inconvenience to you in scheduling. Please feel free to contact us to discuss any conflicts you may have.

Frequently, clients and witnesses ask us, "What should I wear?" Court is a somber, conservative, and noncolorful environment, so the dress should be consistent with that.

Courts have a similar security requirement to airline travel. Do not bring weapons, guns, knives, or mace to court. Some courts do not permit cell phones or purses, so leave them at home or in your car.

While you are in court, please remain quiet. Do not react to the testimony and goings-on. Do not show your feelings, laugh or cry excessively, or become angry. Do not make faces. The court conducts these trials every day and does not want to hear commentary from the audience.

There is a rule of court called the "rule of sequestration," or "the rule." This rule excludes witnesses from the courtroom until they have testified. It is designed to prevent witnesses from tailoring their testimony based on what has transpired in the courtroom. Do not discuss courtroom proceedings with witnesses who have not testified.

When you are in the hallways of the courthouse or elsewhere in public, please do not discuss the case. When the case is concluded and a decision is made, please do not react to the verdict. When the trial is over, quietly gather where we are with our client. We will tell you a little about what has happened and then disburse without incident.

Many times, the judge will make a decision. Other times, the court will "take the matter under advisement" and decide the case another day, after taking time to review the evidence and law. Once the court makes a decision, it is then up to the lawyers to draft a proper order. This usually takes many days.

We look forward to speaking with you soon.

Evidentiary Tools for Trial

The Rules of Evidence, coupled with the tools of discovery, provide excellent tools for ensuring the admissibility of documentary evidence. The paralegal should be familiar with these rules, particularly Rule 902 of the Rules of Evidence entitled "Evidence That Is Self-Authenticating" and Rule 1006 of the Rules of Evidence, which allows for "Summaries to Prove Content."

When subpoenas duces tecum are issued to third parties such as employers, banks, stockbrokers, credit card companies, and the like, an affidavit of authenticity should be provided with the subpoena. When the respondent provides the subpoena response, along with the executed affidavit, the documents are then "self-authenticated" for admission into evidence. A notice of the intent to use the documents as "self-authenticating" should then be served on opposing counsel pursuant to Rule 902(11) along with a copy of the records and affidavit certifying the records, or the records are not self-authenticating. Such a notice, unless disputed for a valid reason, will almost guarantee the admission of the documents.

Usually, documents subpoenaed from third parties, such as banks and credit card companies, must be summarized in order to clarify the point that is to be made. Rule 1006 allows for the admission of such summaries to prove the content of voluminous writings, recordings, or photographs that cannot be conveniently examined in court as long as you make the original or duplicates available to the opposing side for examination or copying at a reasonable time and place. You should also be prepared to produce the documents you are summarizing in court. Although not required, it is good practice to file a *Notice of Service of Summary under Rule 1006* and to list the documents being summarized along with a copy of the summary. This notice should be served in a sufficient time in advance of trial to give the other side the opportunity to review.

Assemble a package for your attorney that includes the *Notice of Service of Summary under Rule 1006*, followed by the *Notice of Intent to Offer Records as Self-Authenticating under Rule 902(11)*, followed by the subpoena duces tecum and the affidavit of records custodian, and then finally the summary and the documents. The attorney then has a great chance of getting all of it admitted into evidence in one move.

IN THE ___________ COURT OF ___________ COUNTY, ___________
___________ JUDICIAL DISTRICT

[NAME OF PLAINTIFF] **PLAINTIFF**

VS. **CAUSE NO. _______________**

[NAME OF DEFENDANT] **DEFENDANT**

STATE OF __________________________
COUNTY OF __________________________

PERSONALLY appeared before me, the undersigned authority in and for the jurisdiction aforesaid, the within named __________________________, [Affiant's Name], who, after being by me first duly sworn, deposes and says as follows:

1. My name is __________________________.
2. I am the records custodian for __________________________. I have firsthand knowledge about the making, maintenance, and storage of documents to which this Affidavit is attached.
3. The documents to which this Affidavit is attached are authentic duplicates of the memoranda, reports, records, and data compilations of acts, events, conditions, opinions, and/or occurrences, made at or near the time of the occurrence of the matters set forth by, or from information transmitted by, a person with knowledge of those matters. These documents are and were made and kept in the course of regularly conducted business activities of __________________________. It was and is the regular practice of __________________________ to make the said memoranda, reports, records, and data compilations.
4. These records are maintained in the form that such records are kept in the regular practice and course of __________________________'s regularly conducted activities.

FURTHER, Affiant saith naught.

____

[PLEASE SIGN]

SWORN TO AND SUBSCRIBED BEFORE ME this the _____ day of ____________, [year].

____

NOTARY PUBLIC

My Commission Expires:

IN THE ___________ COURT OF ___________ COUNTY, ___________
___________ JUDICIAL DISTRICT

[NAME OF PLAINTIFF] **PLAINTIFF**

VS. **CAUSE NO. _______________**

[NAME OF DEFENDANT] **DEFENDANT**

NOTICE OF INTENT TO OFFER RECORDS AS SELF-AUTHENTICATING UNDER RULE 902(11)

PLEASE TAKE NOTICE that pursuant to Rule 902(11) of the Rules of Evidence, counsel for the [Plaintiff/Defendant], ______________________, intends to offer the records that were received from ______________________, as self-authenticating at the trial of this matter. A copy of such records, along with their authenticating certificates, have been provided to counsel for the [Plaintiff/Defendant], ______________________, via email on [date]: **Bates Numbered Documents [Bates Numbers of Documents]**.

This the _____ day of ____________, [year].

Respectfully submitted,
[CLIENT'S NAME]

By: /s/Attorney Name
Attorney Name

Attorney Name
Firm Name
Address of Firm Line 1
Address of Firm Line 2
Telephone
Telecopier
Email Address
Attorneys for [Client Name]

CERTIFICATE OF SERVICE

The undersigned counsel does hereby certify that this day a true and correct copy of the foregoing instrument was delivered, via ________, to opposing counsel.

SO CERTIFIED, this the _____ day of ____________, [year].

/s/Attorney Name
Attorney Name

IN THE __________ COURT OF __________ COUNTY, __________
__________ JUDICIAL DISTRICT

[NAME OF PLAINTIFF] **PLAINTIFF**

VS. **CAUSE NO. ____________**

[NAME OF DEFENDANT] **DEFENDANT**

NOTICE OF SERVICE OF SUMMARY UNDER RULE 1006

PLEASE TAKE NOTICE that pursuant to Rule 1006 of the Rules of Evidence, counsel for the [Plaintiff/Defendant], ____________________, intends to present all records that were received from ____________________ in the form of the attached summary due to the voluminous nature of the documents. The original documents have been provided to counsel for the [Plaintiff/Defendant], ____________________, via email on [date].

This the ____ day of __________, [year].

Respectfully submitted,
[CLIENT'S NAME]

By: /s/Attorney Name
Attorney Name

Attorney Name
Firm Name
Address of Firm Line 1
Address of Firm Line 2
Telephone
Telecopier
Email Address
Attorneys for [Client Name]

CERTIFICATE OF SERVICE

The undersigned counsel does hereby certify that this day a true and correct copy of the foregoing instrument was delivered, via ________, to opposing counsel.

SO CERTIFIED, this the _____ day of ____________, [year].

/s/Attorney Name
Attorney Name

The "What We Want" Exhibit

Clarity of presentation is critical. Even though the proof might indicate what your client wants, it is good policy to work with your attorney and the client to develop a concise statement of the relief that is being requested. This can be presented at the end of the client's testimony to give the court a clear picture of exactly what the client wants.

Another benefit of the "What We Want" exhibit is that it helps the attorney and client plot exactly what relief is being requested. For example, there can be occasions where an attorney thinks she or he is presenting all proof of what the client wants and then, after trial, the client asks the attorney why a certain request hadn't been made. If the attorney works with the client on the "What We Want" list, it helps ensure that the proof is structured to request everything the client wants.

What [Client Name] Wants

- Sole Legal and Physical Custody of JRS and JMS
- [Name of Opposing Party]'s Visitation as Set Forth in the Temporary Order
- Child Support (At Least $400 per Child)
- Half of Child Care Costs (Currently $576 per Month)
- Half of the Children's Insurance Premium and Half of Noncovered Medical Expenses for the Minor Children
- Retrieve Her Possessions

Trial Exhibits

A best practice—if not a requirement—is that an attorney have a copy of every evidentiary document for the court and for opposing counsel. Find out from your attorney what documents he or she intends to use and the likely order. It is best to make a document list. Ideal practice is to have each document numbered at the bottom by a Bates stamp and an indication of when the document was served on opposing counsel. (Opposing counsel can be bad about trying to say they didn't receive a document.) Once the documents are determined, make at least five copies, one to put into evidence, one for the judge, one for the witness, one for opposing counsel, and one for your attorney. The documents should be placed in a properly labeled folder. The folders should then be placed in a red rope expandable folder in the order of their proposed admission into evidence.

Courts and judges handle documents differently. Some judges want documents premarked. This means that you will have to cooperate with opposing counsel's staff to make arrangements prior to trial for prenumbering the documents. In addition, you should find out how the judge or court reporter wants the documents numbered. Some prefer that the documents be identified by party, such as P-1 for a plaintiff's document or D-1 for a defendant's document. On the other hand, some judges don't want the designation and prefer documents be numbered consecutively without identification of which party proffered the document.

Some courts might also require that counsel cooperate with each other to identify which documents can be admitted without objection and which cannot. If that is the case, documents can be numbered and a list of documents prepared identifying which documents are admitted and which have been marked for identification only.

Prepare the Order before Court

It has been said, "Prepare your decree before you go to court. That way you will be certain of what you are trying to achieve." This is a great rule. So, work with your attorney in advance of any hearing, motion, or trial to prepare an order that sets forth the desired result. This will focus the preparation efforts.

In addition to focusing the preparation efforts, preparing an order in advance gives you the option of getting the order signed by the court at the hearing. Adjustments may be necessary, so take a tablet or laptop with the form order with you. The benefit of this is that the order is entered immediately and there is no wait. Another very important benefit is that it eliminates the problems of working out the language of the order with the other attorney. If you don't leave a hearing with an order, there is often trouble with the opposing attorney over language, thus necessitating a return to court.

What to Take to Trial

Careful thought and preparation should go into what you take to trial. Here are some items to consider:

Rolling Cart. There is no point in lugging briefcases or bank boxes around when you can load everything up in a rolling cart. Just about everything needed for a day of trial can be packed into such a cart. We use a collapsible rolling crate that costs less than $75.

Supply Box. This is like a fishing tackle box. Put all supplies you might need for trial in there such as paper clips, highlighters, pens, sticky notes, jump drives, exhibit labels, etc. **Mints are an absolute must for any trial!**

Cooler. Purchase a small cooler with places to store water and snacks and other items for the attorneys and client. Ask the attorneys what they would like in the cooler.

Laptop and Cords. Always take an extra laptop and all of the cords needed for use and charging.

Briefcase-Packing Checklist

- Entire case file. Double-check to make sure latest correspondence and pleadings have been updated. Put all emails and phone notes in the file. This can be a paper or digital file depending on your firm's needs.
- Documents for trial (at least five copies of each!)
- Rules of procedure/evidence
- Trial notebook
- Charged laptop/printer/extra cartridges
- Laptop charger
- Legal pads/paper
- Exhibit stickers
- Business cards
- Three-ring notebook paper
- Three-hole punch
- Highlighters (multiple colors)
- Sticky notes (small and large)
- Calculator
- Three pens (at least)
- Stapler/staple puller
- White-out
- Paper clips (multiple sizes)
- Snacks/water
- Mints
- Aspirin or Tylenol
- Jump drives/flash drives

Tracking Trial Exhibits

It is important to track the introduction of exhibits into evidence. The attorney is often quite preoccupied with questioning witnesses and is not in as good a position as the paralegal to track the introduction of exhibits into evidence. Work with your attorney to develop a list of documents that will be offered into evidence, in the proposed order of introduction. Use a trial exhibit tracking ledger to keep track of the offering into evidence of the documents. This process is important for several reasons. One, it helps the attorney make sure that important documents have actually been admitted into evidence. Two, it helps the attorney refer to exhibits during her or his questioning or argument. Three, it helps for posttrial pleadings such as proposed findings of fact or motions for reconsideration.

IN THE ___________ COURT OF ___________ COUNTY, ___________
___________ JUDICIAL DISTRICT

[NAME OF PLAINTIFF] **PLAINTIFF**

VS. **CAUSE NO. _______________**

[NAME OF DEFENDANT] **DEFENDANT**

[DEFENDANT/PLAINTIFF]'S EXHIBIT LIST

Exhibit #	Exhibit Description	Bates #	Admitted	ID Only

Trial Diary

During hearings and trials, take notes of the proceedings in addition to keeping track of documents coming into evidence on a separate document tracking sheet. Talk to your lawyer about what is important to him or her for this, but notes should include the following:

Start and Stop Times. Write down the time proceedings start. For example, "John's direct—9:15." When the direct stops, write the time of the conclusion. If there is a recess, note the time it starts and ends. When cross starts, note the time it starts and ends. When proceedings end at the end of the hearing, note the time. For multiday trials, note the date. There are many occasions where trials take place over several dates at different times, and it is good to keep track of that.

Testimony. Make notes of the testimony. Some people can type fast enough to just about keep a transcript, and that is good but not a must. The important thing is to note key testimony. If the opposing party makes a key admission, make a note. If the opposing party makes a statement that should probably be rebutted, make a note of that and flag it in the journal as something to deal with. The important thing is to keep a record as the matter proceeds of good points made and bad points to deal with.

Objections. Make note of objections by the lawyers and the rulings of the court. For example, "Objection by opposing counsel to hearsay on client's testimony about medical records, sustained by the judge." This can help the lawyer review whether to come back to a point another way and can also help in a motion to reconsider at the conclusion of the trial.

Flagging Key Testimony. It is good to draw a line down the right side of the page with just enough room to make a note about the testimony. You might make a note in the margin or put a star. This can help on keeping track of matters to cover on cross or redirect or rebuttal.

Judge's Questions or Statements. Judges will insert themselves in the trial with comments or questions for attorneys or witnesses. These comments and questions can be a key to the judge's thinking on the case and should be duly noted and flagged. Judges will also give directions or make rulings on things that should be recorded.

Index

A

Abacuslaw, 42
ABA Technology, 42
absence of an attorney, 44
administration
  absence of an attorney, 44
  asset list, 26–29
  client intake, 6–14
  complaint, what to do with, 31–35
  confidentiality, 15–17
  contact information management, 18
  documents, instructing client on how to send, 30
  email pitfalls, 23
  hearing cancellation, 36
  intake questionnaire, 11–14
  referral source thank you letters, 22
  scheduling, 20
  sending large files, 37–40
  setting up a file, 19
  taking over a case from another attorney, 21
  technology resources, 41–43 (*see also* case management software)
Adobe Document Cloud, 37, 39–40
Adobe Scan, 30
advanced certification, 3
Advanced Certified Paralegal (ACP) designation, 3
adverse parties, subpoena of, 165
adverse witnesses, 165, 173
after trial tips, 175
AIA Contract Documents, 42
alternate payee, in QDRO, 61
Amicus Attorney, 42
appraisals, in trial preparation, 169
arrival time, for trial, 171
asset list, 26–29
  first-class asset list, 26
  five-star asset list, 26
  sample asset list and division, 27
  sample asset list and liability list with competing values of parties, 28
  sample asset list and liability list with competing values of parties and client's proposed division, 29
asset notebook, for trial preparation, 164
associate degree, 3
attire, for trial, 171
attorney-client contract, 16
attorney-client privilege, 15
auto loans of adverse party, subpoena of, 165

B

bachelor's degree, 3
bank accounts, 54
bank information documents, from client with child(ren), 50
bank subpoena, sample of, 85–89
banks of adverse party, subpoena of, 165
Bates numbering documents, 79–84
Bates numbers log, creating, 83–84
best practices
  for discovery, 69–70
  for paralegals related to privilege, 24
  for a written contract or memorandum of understanding, 19
Blumberg Excelsior, 42
breaches of confidentiality, tips for avoiding, 24–25
briefcase-packing checklist, for trial, 188
budget section of financial statements, tips for preparing, 50
burial plots, 54
business documents, from client with child(ren), 52
business interests, 54

C

calendaring
  deposition preparation, 71
  software for, 41, 42
  for trial preparation, 137
CallHippo, 43
Capterra, 43
case intake, 8
case management software, 41–43
  functions of
    calendaring, 41
    case management, 41
    contact management, 41
    document assembly, 41, 42
    intake, 41
    referral source management, 41
    time keeping, 41

case management software *(continued)*
importance of, 41–42
collaboration between caseworkers, 42
creates reports, 41
in deadline management and calendaring, 42
increases productivity, 41
listed on ABA Technology website, 42
purpose of, 41
voice recognition, 43
case screening, 8
cellular carrier subpoena, sample of, 90–93
certification, 3
Certified Paralegal exam, 3
child(ren)
documents needed from client with, 50–52
related expense documents, 51
testimony of, 173
child support calculation, 162
client intake, 6–14
case intake, 8
case screening, 8
conflict and confidentiality issues, 10
conflict checking, 8
initial call or contact, 6
questionnaire, 10, 11–14, 22
script, 6–7, 8, 9
tips, 10
clients. *see also* preparing client and witnesses for trial; trial tips for clients
confidentiality
attorney-client privilege, 15
practical tips for protecting client confidences, 24–25
instructing on how to send documents, 30
notice of temporary hearing, 132, 133–134
preparation interviews, 164
client with child(ren), documents needed from, 50–52
bank information, 50
business, 52
child(ren)-related expenses, 51
debts, 51
estate plans, will, or trusts, 51
expenses, 50
financial information, 51
income, 50
investments, 52
real estate, 51
retirement and other benefits, 52
vehicles, 52
Clio, 42
closing, in trial notebook, 168
collaboration between caseworkers, software for, 42
complaint, what to do with, 31
sample complaint form, 32–35
conduct
of the attorneys, 175
in the courthouse, 175
of family at trail, 134, 170
at trial, 172
confidentiality, 15–17
attorney-client privilege, 15
best practices for paralegals related to privilege, 24
breaches of, tips for avoiding, 24–25
practical tips for protecting client confidences, 24–25
rule of confidentiality, 15, 16–17
conflict and confidentiality issues, 10
conflict checking, 8
consultation, 6, 8, 10, 55
contact information management, 18
contact management, software for, 41
Contract Express, 42
cooler, for trial, 188
correspondence, in document preparation, 46
court administrator, 19, 36, 132, 137, 166
court personnel, at trial, 175
CPAs of adverse party, subpoena of, 165
CP designation, 3
create list of orders and elements of each order, 166
credit report, 55
cross-examination, 173
cryptocurrency, 55
cut and paste, in drafting pleadings, 47

D

D3—Dynamic Document Drafting by Microsystems, 42
deadline management, software for, 42
DealBuilder by Business Integrity, 42
debts of client with child(ren), documents concerning, 51
deposition preparation calendaring, 71
depositions
in discovery, 68
at trial, 171
in witness preparation, 164
Descript, 43
direct examination, 173
DirectLaw, 42

discovery
  Bates numbering documents, 79–84
  best practices and tips, 69–70
  deposition preparation calendaring, 71
  depositions, 68
  interrogatories, 68
  requests for documents, 68
  samples
    bank subpoena, 85–89
    cellular carrier subpoena, 90–93
    counseling records subpoena, 94–97
    deposition subpoena, 98–99
    doctor records subpoena, 100–103
    employer subpoena, 104–107
    notice of deposition, 108–109
    notice of inspection, 110–111
    notice of supplemental discovery, 112–113
    pharmacy records subpoena, 114–117
    police department records subpoena, 118–121
    private investigator subpoena, 122–125
    school subpoena, 126–129
    subpoenas duces tecum form, 73–78
  subpoenas duces tecum, 68
    sample form, 73–78
    UIDDA's application to, 72
  types of, 68
discovery check, for trial preparation, 166
discovery supplementation check—30 days out, 166
divorce
  agreement, drafting, 57–59
  agreement checklist, 57–59
  agreement completion checklist, 56
  entry of agreed, 60
DL Drafting Libraries document assembly, 42
document assembly software, for drafting pleadings, 47
document preparation
  correspondence, 46
  divorce agreement checklist, 57–59
  divorce agreement completion checklist, 56
  divorce entry checklist, 60
  entry of agreed divorce, 60
  financial statements, 49–52
    initial documents needed from client with child(ren), 50–52
    tips for preparing budget section, 50
    tips for preparing financial declarations, 49
  pleadings
    drafting, 47
    error checklist, 48
  pleadings, drafting, 47
    cut and paste, 47
    document assembly software, 47
  QDRO basics, 61–66
  Social Security numbers and, 50
document preparation checklist, 53–55
  bank accounts, 54
  burial plots, 54
  business interests, 54
  credit report, 55
  cryptocurrency, 55
  estate or trust interests, 54
  hearing for temporary relief, 55
  history of marriage, 55
  life insurance, 54
  medical insurance, 54
  monthly trade credits/statement of account, 55
  mortgage, 53
  net worth statements, 53
  previous marriage, 54
  real estate appraisal, 53
  real estate—legal description, 53
  retirement accounts, 53
  retirement plan, 53
  safe deposit box, 55
  securities, 54
  statement of expenses, 55
  tax returns, 53
  written agreements, 55
documents
  Bates numbering, 79–84
  evidentiary, 186
  instructing client on how to send, 30
  needed from client with child(ren), 50–52
  requests for, in discovery, 68
  "self-authenticated," 178
  software for assembling, 41, 42
  for temporary hearing, 133
  in trial notebook, 167
  in trial preparation, 169
drafting pleadings, 47
Dragon Professional Individual, 43
dress rehearsals, for trial preparation, 171
Dropbox, 37–40

E

earnings and losses, in QDRO, 62
eavesdropping, 15

email pitfalls, 23
Employee Retirement Income Security Act (ERISA), 61
employer of adverse party, subpoena of, 165
employer subpoena, sample of, 104–107
entry of agreed divorce, 60
Entry of Appearance, 21, 31, 32
estate or trust interests, 54
estate plans of client with child(ren), documents concerning, 51
ethical duty of confidentiality, 16–17
events, monitoring in absence of an attorney, 44
evidentiary tools for trial, 178–184
  Notice of Intent to Offer Records as Self-Authenticating under Rule 902(11), 178, 181–182
  Notice of Service of Summary under Rule 1006, 178, 183
Exari, 42
exhibits. *see* trial exhibits
expense documents, from client with child(ren), 50
expert disclosure, 166
expert witnesses, 68, 135, 136, 166, 170

F

facts, in trial notebook, 167
fact sheet, 163
false evidence, 17
family emergency, in absence of an attorney, 44
family support
  for temporary hearing, 134
  in trial preparation, 170
fees
  for adverse witnesses, 165
  attorney's
    authority for setting, 2, 44
    in drafting a divorce agreement, 59
    scheduling a consultation and, 10
    written contract or memorandum of, 19
  filing, 44
  QDRO processing, 62
files
  return of, in absence of an attorney, 44
  sending large, 37–40
  setting up, 19
final client preparation interview, 164
financial declarations, tips for preparing, 49
financial information of client with child(ren), documents concerning, 51
financial matters, in absence of an attorney, 44
financial statements, preparation of, 49–52
  initial documents needed from client with child(ren), 50–52
  tips for preparing budget section, 50
  tips for preparing financial declarations, 49
first-class asset list, 26
five-star asset list, 26

H

hearing cancellation, 36
hearing for temporary relief, 55
HotDocs, 42, 47

I

impeaching a witness, 171
income of client with child(ren), documents concerning, 50
individual retirement accounts (IRAs), 53
initial call or contact, 6
intake
  questionnaire, 10, 11–14, 22
  software for, 41
interim case management file audit, 135–136
interim trial management, 135–136
interrogatories, 68
interviews, for trial preparation, 165
investments of client with child(ren), documents concerning, 52
issues list for judge, creating, 166

J

judges
  contact information for, 18, 19
  create issues list for, 166
  entry of agreed divorce and, 60
  financial statements and, 49
  hearing for temporary relief and, 55
  questions or statements by, 173, 191
  research memorandums or "trial brief" given to, 170
  ruling made by, 175
  settlement on the day of trial and, 172
  temporary hearings and, 133, 134
  testimony and, 173–174
    of children, 173
  trial exhibits and, 186

K

key dates, in trial preparation, 170
  10 days from trial, 170
  30 days from trial, 170
  60 days from trial, 170
  final days, 170
key testimony in trial diary, flagging, 191

L

laptop and cords, for trial, 188
leading questions, 173
letter or email notifying client of trial, 169–171. *see also* preparing client and witnesses for trial
life insurance, 54
LylySpeech, 43

M

marriage, checklists for
  history of marriage, 55
  previous marriage, 54
McBurney, Emily, 61
medical insurance, 54
memorandum of understanding, 19
mileage and fees for adverse witnesses, subpoenas for, 165
monthly trade credits/statement of account, 55
mortgage, 53
My Case, 42

N

National Association of Legal Assistants (NALA), 3
National Association of Legal Professionals (NALS), 3
National Federation of Paralegal Associations (NFPA), 3
net worth statements, 53
notebooks
  temporary hearing, 134
  trial, 166 (*see also* trial notebook requirements)
notice of deposition, sample of, 108–109
notice of inspection, sample of, 110–111
Notice of Intent to Offer Records as Self-Authenticating under Rule 902(11), 178, 181–182
Notice of Service of Summary under Rule 1006, 178, 183
notice of supplemental discovery, sample of, 112–113

O

objections, in trial diary, 191
opposing counsel
  contact information for, 18
  divorce agreement and, 57
  email pitfalls and, 23
  expert witnesses identified to, 170
  family's behavior towards, 134, 170
  notifying of inadvertent disclosure, 24
  notifying of substituting a counsel, 21
  objections by, in trial diary, 191
  questions asked by, preparation for, 170, 171, 173–174
  "self-authenticated" documents and, 178
  serving trial documents to, 82, 170, 186
  setting depositions and, 70
  trial exhibits and, 186
order of proof, 173
order of questioning, 173

P

paralegal
  certified, 3
  defined, 2
  duties of, 2
Paralegal Advanced Competency Examination (PACE), 3
participant, in QDRO, 61
payment. *see* fees
PCLaw, 42
perjury, 17, 49
personal property
  temporary hearing and, 134
  in trial preparation, 170
pharmacy records subpoena, sample of, 114–117
plan to which QDRO applies, 61
pleadings
  drafting, 47
  error checklist, 48
pleadings check, 166
police department records subpoena, sample of, 118–121
Practice Panther, 42
preliminary client preparation interview, 164
preparing client and witnesses for trial, 169–177
  appraisals, 169
  depositions, 164
  documents, 169
  family support, 170
  key dates, 170
  letter or email notifying client of trial, 169–171
  personal property, 170
  preliminary client preparation interview, 164
  temporary hearing, 133
  time and place, 169
  trial notebook, 170
  trial subpoenas, 165
  witnesses, 169
pretrial, in trial notebook, 167

private investigator subpoena, sample of, 122–125
processing fees, QDRO, 62
production meetings, in absence of an attorney, 44
productivity, software for increasing, 41
Professional Paralegal (PP) exam and designation, 3
PROLaw Ready, 42
proof, order of, 173

Q

qualified domestic relations order (QDRO), 61–66
  alternate payee, 61
  earnings and losses, 62
  participant, 61
  plan to which order applies, 61
  processing fees, 62
  sample form, 63–66
  surviving spouse benefits, 62
  valuation date, 61
questions
  cross-examination, 173
  direct examination, 173
  leading, 173
  by opposing counsel, 170, 171, 173–174
  order of questioning, 173
  redirect, 173
  suggested, for trial, 171
  in trial diary, 191

R

real estate
  appraisal, 53
  documents, from client with child(ren), 51
  legal description, 53
rebuttal, 173, 191
rebuttal witnesses, 168
redirect, 173, 191
referral source management, software for, 41
referral source thank you letters, 22
Registered Paralegal (RP), 3
reports, software for creating, 41
research, in trial notebook, 168
retirement accounts, 53
retirement and other benefits of client with child(ren), documents concerning, 52
retirement plan, 53
rolling cart, for trial, 188
rule of confidentiality, 15, 16–17
rule of sequestration, 174
Rules of Professional Conduct, 15, 16–17
ruling, 175

S

safe deposit box, 55
samples
  asset list and division, 27
  asset list and liability list with competing values of parties, 28
  asset list and liability list with competing values of parties and client's proposed division, 29
  bank subpoena, 85–89
  cellular carrier subpoena, 90–93
  complaint form, 32–35
  counseling records subpoena, 94–97
  deposition subpoena, 98–99
  doctor records subpoena, 100–103
  employer subpoena, 104–107
  notice of deposition, 108–109
  notice of inspection, 110–111
  notice of supplemental discovery, 112–113
  pharmacy records subpoena, 114–117
  police department records subpoena, 118–121
  private investigator subpoena, 122–125
  QDRO form, 63–66
  school subpoena, 126–129
  subpoenas duces tecum form, 73–78
scheduling, 20
school subpoena, sample of, 126–129
script, for client intake, 6–7, 8, 9
securities, 54
security, at trial, 172
"self-authenticated" documents, 178
sending large files, 37–40
sequestration, 174
setting of case for trial, checking, 166
setting up a file, 19
settlement on the day of trial, 172
"60-day deadline for expert witnesses," 135
Social Security numbers, on documents, 50
software. *see* case management software
Sonix, 43
SpeakEZ, 43
start and stop times, in trial diary, 191
statement of expenses, 55
statements, in trial diary, 191
STI PracticeMaster, 42
subpoenas duces tecum
  in discovery, 68
  sample subpoenas duces tecum form, 73–78
  UIDDA's application to, 72
supplementation, 166, 170
supply box, for trial, 188
support, at trial, 175

supporting financial documents and related information. *see* document preparation checklist
surprise witnesses, 168
surviving spouse benefits, in QDRO, 62

T

taking over a case from another attorney, 21
taking the stand, 173
tax returns, 50, 52, 53, 54, 55, 174
technology resources, 41–43. *see also* case management software
temporary hearing, 132–134
- checklist, 132
- documents, 133
- family support, 134
- issues at, 133
- nature of, 133
- notebook, 134
- notice to client of temporary hearing, 132, 133–134
- personal property, 134
- preparation, 134
- procedures, 133
- witnesses, 133

temporary hearing checklist, 132
temporary hearing notebook, 134
testifying, tips for, 173–174
testimony
- of children, 173
- judges and, 173–174
- in trial diary, 191

time and place, for trial, 169
time keeping, software for, 41
Time Matters, 42
tips
- for discovery, 69–70
- for preparing financial documents, 49–50
- for protecting client confidences, 24–25
- trial tips for clients, 171–176

Transkriptor, 43
trial
- calendaring for trial preparation, 137
- checklists (*see* trial preparation checklist)
- child support calculation, 162
- evidentiary tools for trial, 178–184
- fact sheet, 163
- interim case management file audit, 135–136
- interim trial management, 135–136
- prepare the order before court, 187
- preparing client and witnesses for (*see* preparing client and witnesses for trial)
- temporary hearing, 132–134
- tips for (*see* trial tips for clients)
- tracking trial exhibits, 189–190
- trial diary, 191
- trial exhibits, 186
- trial notebook, 166, 167–168
- trial preparation overview, 164–166 (*see also* trial preparation checklist)
- trial prep checklist, 138–140
- what to take to trial, 188
- "what we want" exhibit, 185

trial diary, 191
trial exhibits, 186
- document list for, 165
- exhibit list, sample of, 190
- tracking, 189–190

trial notebook, 166
trial notebook requirements, 167–168
- closing, 168
- documents, 167
- facts, 167
- other witnesses, 168
- pretrial, 167
- research, 168
- witnesses in order of appearance, 167–168
- witness list, 167

trial preparation checklist, 138–140, 164–166
- asset notebook, 164
- check setting of case for trial, 166
- create issues list for judge, 166
- create list of orders and elements of each order, 166
- discovery check, 166
- discovery supplementation check—30 days out, 166
- exhibits, 165
- expert disclosure, 166
- final client preparation interview, 164
- interviews, 165
- pleadings check, 166
- preliminary client preparation interview, 164
- send witness list to client
- subpoenas, 165
- trial notebook, 166
- "what we want" list, 166
- witnesses, 166
- witness preparation, 164

trial subpoenas, 165
trial tips for clients, 171–176
- after trial, 175
- children testifying, 173
- conduct at trial, 172
- conduct in the courthouse, 175

trial tips for clients *(continued)*
conduct of the attorneys, 175
court personnel, 175
depositions, 171
dress rehearsals, 171
order of proof, 173
order of questioning, 173
preparation, 171
ruling, 175
security, 172
sequestration, 174
suggestions, 171
support, 175
taking the stand, 173
testifying, 173–174
what happens when you get there?, 172
what to wear, 171
when to arrive, 171
winning, 175–176
witnesses, 172
trust, 54
trusts of client with child(ren), documents concerning, 51
Twilio, 43

U

Uniform Interstate Depositions and Discovery Act (UIDDA), 72

V

valuation date, in QDRO, 61
vehicles of client with child(ren), documents concerning, 52
voice recognition software, 43

W

waiver of disclosure of confidential information, 16
"what we want" exhibit, 185
"what we want" list, 166
wills of client with child(ren), documents concerning, 51
winning, at trial, 175–176
witnesses. *see also* preparing client and witnesses for trial
adverse, 165, 173
expert, 68, 135, 136, 166, 170
impeaching, 171
"may call," 164
rebuttal, 168
sequestration, 174
subpoena of, 165
surprise, 168
in trial notebook
order of appearance, 167–168
other, 168
"will call," 164
witness list
sending to client, 165
in trial notebook, 167–168
written agreements, 55